Building Democracy in Eritrea

Conference at Senate House, London, 24–25 April 2019

Conference Record

Exposing Human Rights Abuses in Eritrea

Published by University of London Press on behalf of the Institute of Commonwealth Studies

University of London Press
Senate House
Malet Street
London
WC1E 7HU
https://sas.ac.uk/publications/

First published 2019

ISBN 978-1-912250-30-1 (paperback edition)

ISBN 978-1-912250-31-8 (PDF edition)

Contents

Group photo of delegates at the conference (Credit: Martin Plaut)

1. Executive summary

Eritrea Focus, in partnership with the Institute of Commonwealth Studies, held a two-day conference titled 'Building Democracy in Eritrea' on 24–25 April 2019 in Senate House, University of London. The conference brought together a range of experts – Eritrean and international – to discuss and begin to think about how a free and democratic Eritrea might emerge in the future, post-dictatorship. Our aim is to play a facilitative role in this process, and to use the conference as an opportunity to look at the challenges currently facing Eritrea, in order to put forward solutions and to assist in the emergence of a democratic government.

Speakers came from a range of backgrounds and offered many viewpoints, which made the event fascinating and thought-provoking. A range of pre-identified thematic areas, including the rule of law, the national economy and the role of women and youth, were discussed.

The conference was opened by Thangam Debbonaire MP, Co-Chair of the All-Party Parliamentary Group on Eritrea, following introductory remarks by the Chair of Eritrea Focus, Habte Hagos. The conference layout allowed for keynote speeches to be delivered, with designated Q&A time to follow, which gave the floor the opportunity to engage with the speakers. The inclusion of breakout sessions for some of the topics (The Rule of Law and Administration of Justice, and The National Economy in an Integrating Region) encouraged more in-depth discussion, as the 70 delegates were split into two groups and participated in stimulating debates surrounding the topics. Day one of the conference came to an end with dinner held at the nearby Antalya restaurant, where delegates were free to engage in more informal discussions and to reflect on the proceedings of the day. Michela Wrong (author and journalist) gave an interesting talk during the meal on her insights into Eritrea.

The conference was brought to a close with a reception at Senate House, which gave delegates and speakers further opportunity to network and reflect together on the event.

'Building Democracy in Eritrea' was designed to be a starting point. Whilst the conference proved incredibly valuable in bringing together, and giving a platform to, prominent speakers and political activists, the discussions that ensued built the foundations for the next steps. We have identified a range of working groups, with carefully selected experts, to take forward the ideas discussed during the conference. The aim of these expert groups is to begin the process of thinking about how Eritrea might be reconstructed post-regime change, based on universal human rights and rule of law.

Whilst the conference was overall successful, we appreciate there may have been some shortfalls. The planning group will assess areas in which we could have performed better, such as ensuring better representation of minority groups, in order to ensure inclusivity, and will incorporate the lessons learned into future events.

This publication brings together in a single document the papers prepared by each of the speakers and the agenda of the conference. The views expressed are those of the authors.

2. Chair's welcome by Habte Hagos

Habte Hagos, founding member and Chair of Eritrea Focus, speaking at the conference (Credit: Martin Plaut)

Dear friends, colleagues and distinguished guests,

Good morning. My name is Habte Hagos. I am the founding member and Chair of Eritrea Focus.

On behalf of Eritrea Focus and the Institute for Commonwealth Studies, I would like to welcome you to the 'Building Democracy in Eritrea' two-day conference. It is great to see you all and welcome to London.

This conference has been organised in partnership with the Institute of Commonwealth Studies, here at the University of London. I would like to thank everyone at the Institute and Senate House for hosting us in this magnificent place.

I would also like to express our gratitude to the National Endowment for Democracy, which has generously supported the conference, allowing us to invite so many of you from around the world.

Friends,

Eritrea is at a crossroads. The peace deal signed with Ethiopia last year may have removed the threat of war, lifting a great weight from the shoulders of the nation. The partial reopening of the border crossings between the two countries has brought an increase in trade and allowed families to be reunited for the first time in decades.

Why, then, do so many Eritreans continue to flee this 'peace'? The vast conscript army, trapped in indefinite national service, has not been demobilised, despite the rapprochement with Ethiopia.

The dust may have been blown from the Ethiopian ambassador's residence in Asmara, but the population remains in the dark about the exact nature of the agreement negotiated by Prime Minister Abiy and President Isaias. The peace process is increasingly being seen – by both Eritreans and Ethiopians – as an agreement between two individuals rather than two nation states.

At the heart of the problem lies the dictatorship. Deprived of the rights enshrined in the UN Charter, the Eritrean people are increasingly angry. With the end of the military threat from Ethiopia, many are asking: 'Why does the road to democracy remain so emphatically blocked?' Demands for change are heard on the streets of Eritrea's towns and villages, and throughout the diaspora. Sadly, however, the people have not seen any sign of change in their constitutional rights, nor their basic human rights – rights that we take for granted here. Countless Eritreans continue to languish in unknown prison cells scattered across the country, without the due process of law. Eritrea has indeed become a prison state for its people.

Progress is blocked by one man: President Isaias. Resistance is increasing, but one key question remains: what will replace him, and the clique that surrounds him, when he has gone? One thing is for sure: we cannot allow a vacuum to develop. The examples of Libya and Iraq are too painful, too stark. We also know that we do not have a moment to waste. There is a real urgency: a need to find a path to a better, brighter future. One that will give us the Eritrea for which so many of our brothers and sisters gave their lives to liberate; a country which we all long for and a country that is at peace with itself and its neighbours.

Over the next two days, we will address this and many other pressing questions about the future of Eritrea. We will reflect upon how independence was won in 1991, and how freedom was lost; how the recent wave of reconciliation throughout the Horn of Africa can be institutionalised and sovereignty guaranteed; what steps are required to rebuild a regionally integrated economy that can fuel growth and prosperity in the country; how to enshrine free speech laws and representation in a vibrant and diverse media environment.

We will consider the unresolved question of the Constitution, and the milestones that must be passed in the transition to democracy; how to rebuild the shattered economy; how Eritreans in the country and throughout the diaspora can strengthen civic organisations and protect social and religious freedoms – the very fabric of Eritrean society that President Isaias has single-handedly destroyed over almost three decades. How can we engage with international democracies to ensure recognition of the plight of Eritrea while safeguarding the primacy of Eritreans in deciding the country's future? In this regard, we have the unfailing support of our international friends, as can be seen around this room. These are the very people who have steadfastly supported the Eritrean people through thick and thin. To you, my friends, I say thank you from the bottom of my heart.

I know that between us we have the experience, insight and imagination to tackle these questions. The papers for this conference will be brought together in a published form and made available to a wider readership. These papers, along with the conclusions of this conference, will serve as a permanent record of what took place here, and will also generate action points that we plan to progress over the coming months with the help of some of you.

I am sure that you will be keen to speak with one another on the fringes of this conference, over dinner this evening and at our post-conference reception tomorrow – when I hope you will be able to join us. We encourage you to make the most of the opportunities you have to renew old acquaintances and cultivate new channels of communication and cooperation. Our hope is that these networks will grow beyond the conference, providing the basis for future meetings, workshops and activities that feed into the process of change.

This is integral to our purpose here. We have amongst us many eminent academics and experts, but the subjects we are discussing are not purely 'academic'. What we will discuss here has a bearing on questions that grow more urgent by the day.

Only this month we have seen, not too far from Eritrea, how long-standing dictatorships are brought down by relentless pressure from the streets. Since 2011, we have seen how precariously these moments hang in the balance if there is no system for a just, accountable and peaceful transition to rule of law and eventual democracy.

The current regime in Eritrea will fall; the narrow foundations on which it is built cannot sustain the weight of its misdeeds.

What is vital is that we lay the foundations of a democratic Eritrea. Our young people are saying: Enough! We must make their vision a reality – so that we can all walk the sands of the Red Sea without fear and drink coffee in Asmara, without looking over our shoulders.

This conference is one step towards that goal.

Thank you.

3. Opening remarks by Thangam Debbonaire MP

Thangam Debbonaire MP, Member of Parliament for Bristol West and Co-Chair of the Eritrea All-Party Parliamentary Group (Credit: Martin Plaut)

Thangam Debbonaire introduced herself as the Co-Chair of the All-Party Parliamentary Group (APPG) on Eritrea and Chair of the APPG on Refugees.

Thangam thanked Eritrea Focus for hosting the conference and delivered an improvised address in which she spoke about the role of APPG officers being to listen to experts and offer an entry point to getting important issues onto the parliamentary agenda.

She also spoke about the recent killing of Northern Irish journalist Lyra McKee, shot during unrest in Londonderry on 18 April 2019, and about how transitions away from long-standing conflicts must constantly be managed and maintained by all parties involved to ensure sustainable peace. She spoke enthusiastically about her sense of privilege at being invited to address a conference that would have a lasting impact on the future of democracy in Eritrea.

Later the same day, Thangam mentioned her attendance at the conference in the House of Commons during a debate on intimidation of candidates standing in the European Parliament elections, emphasising the need to maintain civil discourse as part of a functioning democracy.

4. Winning independence and governing a state: missed opportunities and lessons learned

Ambassador Haile Menkerios

Former Eritrean ambassador to the African Union and UN Secretary General's special envoy to Sudan and South Sudan

[Message of support sent to the conference and read in its entirety on Haile Menkerios's behalf by Paulos Tesfagiorgios]

Dear organisers of and participants in the conference on democracy in Eritrea,

Let me start by expressing regret for my inability to participate in the conference due to unforeseen but critical engagements for the peaceful resolution of conflicts within the Horn of Africa region.

It is indeed timely to discuss the need for building democracy in Eritrea, a country which has the notoriety of being perhaps the only country in Africa that does not have a functioning constitution, a legitimate/elected government, nor legitimate and functioning governance institutions that ensure accountability. Since gaining independence, Eritrea has been ruled by a militaristic one-man dictatorship that believes in using confrontation to resolve conflicts/disputes with its neighbours rather than legal means and dialogue. In fact, Eritrea has also the notoriety of being the only country in Africa to have been at war, directly or indirectly, at some time or another, with every one of its neighbours!

Generally speaking, other liberation movements that won independence or liberation through an armed struggle have also established one-party dictatorships with varying degrees of accountability to the general public. A key characteristic of the political parties that were established by these movements is that they controlled armies, police and justice institutions, and it was these institutions that also became institutions of the state. The distinction between the institution of the party, the government and the state disappeared. In such countries, building democracy with public institutions independent of direct control by political parties is an outcome that is yet to materialise. In this, Eritrea is perhaps unique only in degrees.

Eritrea's particular history and experience of decolonisation has contributed to the unique nature of governance that has been established there – a one-man rather than one-party dictatorship. The basis for this was, in my opinion, the nature of the struggle we had to wage: a struggle against a much bigger and stronger Ethiopia supported by the African continent and both the West and the East – a peculiar characteristic. The enemy we had to fight was so formidable that getting rid of it consumed the major part of our energy, and we did not exert much effort to adequately plan and prepare for what and how to build once our enemy was defeated. Indeed, we built a very efficient fighting machine in the EPLF with absolute discipline and a hierarchical system as an effective military.

Despite the prevailing rhetoric during the struggle, the EPLF did not encourage debate and discussion to develop concrete ideas about our future after independence and establish institutions or safeguards to ensure their implementation. What was our strength during the struggle thus became our weakness after independence. For better or for worse, those of us who participated in the heroic struggle of the Eritrean people for independence contributed to the development of the dictatorship we have now.

One can perhaps see a parallel in the Arab Spring, where people were united against very formidable regimes determined to destroy what they hated, but did not spend enough time and energy to articulate and organise for what they wanted to replace them by. The result has been somewhat similar – even worse (chaos) in some situations.

I believe that in building democracy in Eritrea, our particular history and its legacy need to be taken into consideration. I would suggest that in thinking about how to move, we consider going back to what we could and should have done in 1991, immediately after liberation: call for a national conference of representatives of the Eritrean people that would decide on a transitional arrangement to ensure an inclusive process of building participatory democracy in the country. I believe only such a process can prevent violence. Such a process has been pursued in other parts of the continent with a fair degree of success, though unfortunately only after violent confrontations with much destruction.

I apologise for the lengthy note of apology and for my inability to attend, but I also wished in doing so to contribute a few ideas to the discussions on building democracy in Eritrea.

I wish you success in your discussions to contribute to this noble initiative.

Paulos Tesfagiorgios

Former Chair of the Eritrean Relief Association and involved in drafting Eritrea's post-independence constitution

Ambassador Haile Menkerios rightly said:

'The enemy we had to fight was so formidable that getting rid of it consumed the major part of our energy, and we did not exert much effort to adequately plan and prepare for what and how to build once our enemy was defeated.'

Indeed, we built a very efficient fighting machine in the EPLF, with absolute discipline and a strict hierarchical structure. A highly effective military apparatus was an absolute necessity not only for our success but also for our survival – there was no other way out, no serious negotiations, etc. The Eritrean struggle for independence thus ended up being the only liberation movement in Africa to win its struggle solely militarily – and I do not need to explain that to this audience.

The EPLF was not only a military organisation, however. It had a civilian side too: health, education, infrastructure, building, agriculture, veterinary services. It also had political side, mobilising and organising the people, etc. It promoted a beautiful vision. A vision of a peaceful, democratic society in which everyone contributed and prospered. It was this vision that its members believed in and fought for, including paying with their lives.

The EPLF Charter pronounces: 'In independent Eritrea, it is our basic desire to build a stable political system which respects law and order, safeguards unity and peace,… guarantees basic human rights, and is free from fear and oppression… a democratic constitutional system based on sovereignty of the people, on democratic principles and procedures, on accountability, transparency, pluralism and tolerance.'

This realisation of the vision depended, absolutely, upon a strong military to deliver independence. And therein lay the fatal contradiction. How does a liberation movement which is so utterly dependent upon its military deliver its vision of a democratic future?

Ambassador Haile continues to lament:

'Despite the prevailing rhetoric during the struggle, the EPLF did not encourage debate and discussion to develop concrete ideas about our future after independence and establish institutions or safeguards to ensure their implementation. What was our strength during the struggle thus became our weakness after independence.'

Immediately following our extraordinary victory, there were important attempts to implement the above vision. The most important being drafting and adopting the 1997 Constitution; drafting election laws; attempts to reform all the then prevailing laws to harmonise them with the new Constitution.

Far from giving way to a new democratic order, however, the culture of absolute obedience and military superiority continued to dominate Eritrean leadership after victory, and all attempts to establish institutions or democratic safeguards essential to making the vision a reality were quashed, and all who tried to champion such moves fled the country, even worse, were brutally suppressed, including incommunicado imprisonment.

Where are we now?

At present, the Eritrean society and economy has virtually disintegrated: the flight of youth across the borders has complicated the demography with huge implications for the economy and social development; the President's 'divide and rule' policies and practices, even amongst his own people, meant absolute one-man rule; openings provided by peace with Ethiopia have been squandered and now the President himself is thoroughly discredited in the eyes of the Eritrean people.

So, what happens when Isaias is no longer on the scene? How can democratic change be instigated, and by whom?

It is important to take the challenges faced, both domestic and foreign.

1.   Domestic issues/challenges:
   - Limited experience with open, democratic dialogue and praxis; fragmented society or social order: ruined economy; paralysed institutions, such as the bureaucracy, judiciary and National Assembly/Parliament.
   - Absence of experience of civic/citizen participation in matters of state policy.
   - Civil servants forced to resort to corruption and contraband to augment their meagre income.
   - Lawlessness, including human trafficking, abounding.
   - A frightening and dangerous situation of desperation, acute contradictions, conflicts and divisions surfacing in the Eritrean society.

2. External/regional complications:
   • We live in a regional dynamic that militates against stability and peace; with strong and deep democratic culture lacking across the region.
   • The current ethnic based tensions, unrest and sporadic eruption of violence in Ethiopia.
   • Continued state weakness in Somalia, ongoing civil war in South Sudan, terrorism, intervention and its spill-over effects in the region.
   • Potential foreign interventions: the Saudis, the UAE, Egypt or even Ethiopia?

All the above can have their impact on the sovereignty of the country with the potential of creating chaos, confusion and violent conflict which might usher in extremism of various types and thwart a smooth transition.

What possible scenarios post-Isaias? Who can take over power from Isaias?

It is impossible to predict what might happen, and why, after Isaias. In general, anything can happen, anytime.

Eritrea faces a situation where freedom of association, expression and exchange of opinion, especially as a group, is absolutely denied, thwarting collective reflection, let alone systematic planning and concrete preparation, for a post-Isaias future.

Under the circumstances, the military alone can take over; *or*, senior military commanders and senior party officials, colluding for self-preservation and for clique or individual survival. However, Eritrea is faced with a military institution that is weak, that is falling apart, that is distrusted by the people and that distrusts each other.

Or, change could be provoked by civil disobedience, despite the fact that organised civilian life is non-existent, with no student groupings or movements, no professional associations and no social clubs.

It is important to note too that the process by which a system is replaced, and the conditions that prevail afterward, often determine the framework and process of a stable transition and democratic governance.

Call for a national conference

Again, Ambassador Haile suggests, in building democracy in Eritrea, that:

'... our particular history and its legacy need to be taken into consideration. I would suggest that in thinking about how to move, we consider going back to what we could and should have done in 1991, immediately after liberation: call for a national conference of representatives of the Eritrean people that would decide on a transitional arrangement to ensure an inclusive process of building participatory democracy in the country. I believe only such a process can prevent violence.'

Ambassador Haile makes a very important suggestion, convening a national conference. However, it is not simple. It raises many questions and requires careful preparations, including practical steps such as:
   • Who can organise such a conference?
   • Who identifies the challenges the national conference will have to engage with?
   • When is the national conference to happen? Presumably, right after the fall of the dictatorship. Or before or after the fall of the dictator? What are the specific goals of such a conference?

In any case, the national conference that Ambassador Haile Menkerios suggests will have to contend with a post-dictatorship and post-conflict complex situation where the following issues are among many:
1. How is a transition from a long period of a state of no-war, no-peace, an authoritarian system, a highly personalised rule and an exclusionist state to a peaceful, stable and democratic polity and an inclusive state where the *rule of law* is supreme to take place?
2. Transition, whether under the national conference, or any other arrangement, will have to look into the construction of the conditions required for democratic governance and an open society to take root by addressing, among other things, the following:
   • Re/establishing a functioning government; building free and fair political rules, systems and institutions; developing civil society; constructing a robust legal infrastructure as well as fostering public confidence in the institutions of government such as the police, the courts and different ministries.
   • Structural institutional patterns that have or might have inevitably arisen from a long and persistent authoritarian/dictatorial rule (rule by the security apparatus).
   • Crimes that have or might have been committed during the period of authoritarian and dictatorial rule; healing potentially lingering hostility and divisions within society so that reconciliation can take place.

- Post-dictatorship issues of safety, security and the well-being and dignity of the citizen.
- The geopolitical realignments in the Horn and their potential impact on a peaceful, orderly and managed transition to stability.
- Militarism.

How to move forward

The old question arises again: are we presently really, adequately, prepared for change? For stable, peaceful, democratic transition? Or are we going to continue to say, 'we could not prepare, as getting rid of the dictatorship consumed all our energies'?

We need to prepare for the eventual and certain change. We need to provide the assembly of citizens or national conference the solid materials they can rely on for their deliberations.

This will mean quickly producing knowledge on various aspects of transition and national life, not just programmes, as many groups seem to have. We need to:

- Develop an analytical framework for key priorities in transition: peace, democracy and development.
- Strengthen citizen groups – the youth and especially women – to engage in stable transitions, transformation, peace, democracy and development at national, sub-regional and regional levels.
- Promote informed public discourse; advance understanding of transitions, peace, building democracy and development.

The challenges are enormous, time is not a luxury that we have. The demand from our people is for immediate results.

5. The rapprochement between Ethiopia and Eritrea

Kjetil Tronvoll

Professor of and research director of Peace and Conflict Studies, Bjørknes University, Oslo

Localising peace: people-to-people reconciliation in the Eritrean-Ethiopian borderlands

Introduction

'Finally, we are once again *one*, as brothers should be', expresses the elderly gentleman I talk to on the streets of Mekelle, the capital of the northern region of Tigray in Ethiopia, a couple of months after the opening of the borders in mid September 2018. The city had been flooded by Eritreans, who, for the first time in 20 years, were free to cross the border to Tigray and Ethiopia. Tales of reunions of long-lost family members and relatives spread like wildfire, and the cross-border trade and business were booming.

The formal peace agreement entered into between Prime Minister Abiy Ahmed of Ethiopia and President Isaias Afwerki of Eritrea in July 2018 launched the start of the bilateral reorientation of relationships from conflict to reconciliation. But bilateral relations need also to be anchored on the ground if reconciliation is to be effective and successful; to localise peace among the people who have suffered during the war.

This short paper will present some observations of people-to-people reconciliation between the Tigrinya-speaking border populations of Eritrean and Ethiopia, building upon fieldwork on the Ethiopian side of the border during shorter periods over the last five years. By way of conclusion, some challenges to establishing durable reconciliation will be highlighted.

The period of estrangement

Wars and conflicts have ravaged the Eritrean-Ethiopian highlands throughout centuries. The 'commoners' have been used as pawns and 'expendables' in the elites' struggle for political power, in historical as well as contemporary wars. As declarations and decisions of war and conflict are made by a small elite at the top of society, without any democratic accountability, people have generally managed to distinguish between the political leaders instigating the war, and ordinary people fighting it. When doing research in Tigray after the outbreak of the 1998–2000 war, an elderly Tigrayan farmer explained this context eloquently:

> When the Eritreans attacked us, we did not know what to believe. We used to think of them as our brothers – we have bonds of marriage, trade, and friendship that link us together. We were also fighting together as one against the military junta. Now, suddenly they have become our mortal enemies; and our old foes, the Amhara, are coming to our rescue! But, although we are fighting the Eritreans today with the help of the Amhara, this may change again tomorrow; as different kings [governments] come and go, so also will our enemies and friends change.[1]

Similar sentiments were also heard among the Eritrean border population when the Ethiopian forces advanced deep into Eritrea in the counter-offensives during the war. Due to this warring history, the highland population of Eritrea and Ethiopia has also had a remarkable capacity to reconcile after conflict, as their common destiny as pawns and victims of war brings them together.

The devastating 1998–2000 war and the subsequent 'no-war, no-peace' stalemate, which entailed a militarisation of the border on both sides, kept the populations physically apart for 20 years. At no other time in history has the Tigrinya-speaking highland population of Tigray and Eritrea been separate for such a long period. War and long-time physical and social separation will eventually lead to a reconfiguration of identities that used to be aligned and considered as affiliated groups. Research recently conducted in a border village on the Ethiopian side informs us that the younger generations have a very different conceptualisation of and identity towards their brethren on the Eritrean side than their parental generations.[2] The physical separation has naturally made an imprint on their understanding of the 'other'

---

1   Quote taken from Tronvoll, K. *War and the Politics of Identity in Ethiopia: The Making of Enemies and Allies in the Horn of Africa* (Woodbridge: James Currey, 2009) pp.1–2.

2   Dias, A.M. 'Borderless World vs Borders as Walls: insights from a borderland group in northern Ethiopia', in Rodrigues, C.U. and Tomàs, J. (eds) *Crossing African Borders* (Lisbon: Centro de Estudos Internacionais, 2012) https://books.openedition.org/cei/222?lang=en

on the other side of the trenches. What used to be conceptualised in terms of 'kinsfolk', are now increasingly considered as 'aliens'.

Due to the long separation and feeling of betrayal on both sides, many Eritreans and Ethiopians were hesitant about the possibilities of future reconciliation between the two peoples. Lacking any representative study, the impression however is that more Eritreans than Ethiopians questioned the possibility to reconcile. This may be due to a number of reasons. For one, the continued occupation of territories granted to Eritrea by Ethiopian forces sustains the image of Ethiopia as a threat to Eritrean sovereignty. But, also, the fact of experienced social and political isolation post-2000, sustained war mobilisation and the lack of access to information and alternative narratives than the officially produced master narrative of PFDJ have their impact. Tigrayans and Ethiopians have, on the other hand, 'moved on' after the war, demobilised, concentrating on development, and facing new challenges and problems domestically; hence the enmity harboured during the war against Eritreans has long since been subdued and disremembered. The restoration and reparation law enacted in Ethiopia some years back, where Eritreans expelled during the war were given back their lost property rights or compensation in Ethiopia, has furthermore shown an official capacity to abolish the 'formal enemy image' produced during the war.

The coming to power of Prime Minister Abiy Ahmed in Ethiopia in April 2018, at the cost of TPLF dominance over the government,[3] turned the page on the formal bilateral relations between Addis and Asmara. PM Abiy reached out to President Isaias Afwerki of Eritrea and asked for peace between the two brotherly people, reassuring him that Ethiopia would respect and implement the Algiers peace agreement and its border demarcation decision. Thereafter, on the symbolic Martyrs' Day of 20 June 2018, President Isaias Afwerki commented on the political changes in Ethiopia and that the 'end of the TPLF's shenanigans' made a peace process with Ethiopia possible.[4] President Isaias's statement underlines the thesis that the war was between political elites – this time between the leaders of Tigray and Eritrea – and that the grassroots have no influence or say in when peace and reconciliation ought to take place.

After a brief period of talks, PM Abiy travelled to Asmara and met for the first time with President Isaias. Together they signed a Joint Declaration of Peace and Friendship between Eritrea and Ethiopia, stating: 'The state of war between Ethiopia and Eritrea has come to an end. A new era of peace and friendship has been opened.'[5] Subsequently, in rapid succession, diplomatic relations and communication lines between the two countries were restored, and soon Ethiopian Airlines commenced regular flights between Addis Ababa and Asmara. Finally, on 11 September, the military trenches were dismantled and President Isaias and PM Abiy opened the border crossings on the ground, and Eritreans and Ethiopians in their thousands crossed into each other's countries to reconnect with friends and family on the other side who they had not seen for 20 years.[6]

Prior to this, however, there had been a gradual process over several years of people-to-people contact and reconciliation on the ground; ignoring and undermining the formal enmity between the two states and governments.

People-to-people reconciliation during war[7]

People-to-people contact and reconciliation has been a continuous subaltern process since 2000, primarily manifested by Eritreans fleeing their country and seeking refuge in Ethiopia. Hundreds of thousands of Eritreans have crossed over to Tigray, despite the officially produced narrative of the Eritrean government portraying Tigrayans as the enemy. As far as I know, not *one* Eritrean has reported harassment or vindictive incidents when they have sought protection on the Ethiopian side of the border; rather the opposite, all informants confirm that they have been well received and offered hospitality by the Tigrayan border population who they have first come into contact with.[8] The informal and formal reception of Eritrean refugees in Tigray is surely an attest of the close affinity between the two people. Both Ethiopian and Tigrayan authorities have gone far beyond the requirements in the Refugee Convention to host and care for their Eritrean brethren. But hosting refugees is not in itself a proof of mutual reconciliation between the peoples living in the two countries. For that to transpire, sustained cross-border social interaction between communities on both sides would need to be established.

---

3   TPLF voted against Abiy Ahmed taking over the chairmanship of EPRDF. See interview with TPLF chair Dr Debretsion in the *Financial Times* https://www.ft.com/content/1cbaac04-457f-11e9-a965-23d669740bfb

4   See transcript of the speech https://www.eastafro.com/2018/06/19/video-2018-eritrea-martyrs-day-commemoration/ President Isaias's statement has been translated differently by different news outlets. For instance, the *Sudan Tribune* attributes Isaias with the words 'TPLF clique, and other vultures'. See http://www.sudantribune.com/spip.php?article65687

5   Joint Declaration of Peace and Friendship between Eritrea and Ethiopia http://www.shabait.com/news/local-news/26639-joint-declara-tion-of-peace-and-friendship-between-eritrea-and-ethiopia

6   https://www.nytimes.com/2018/09/11/world/africa/ethiopia-eritrea-border-opens.html

7   While there is no official or standardised definition of 'People-to-People' (P2P), most generally agree that it entails bringing together representatives of conflicting groups to interact purposefully in a safe space ('People-to-people Peacebuilding: A Program Guide' (Washington DC: USAID, 2011) p.5.

8   There are several incidents of grievances expressed by Eritrean refugees in the official camps in Tigray, relating to various issues of malad-ministration. These incidents are not, however, related to vindictive sentiments by the Tigrayan population.

As in any war or conflict zone, contraband activities are the first activities undertaken across the no-man's land, and so also between Eritrea and Ethiopia. Early on, information about petty trade and smuggling activities was heard; although this cannot be an indicator of people-to-people reconciliation. The first incidents in such regard were a number of non-refugee Eritreans crossing over to Tigray and later returning to Eritrea to participate in the annual Maryam Zion religious festival in Axum.[9] Already, in 2009, we have information about Eritreans participating in this religious celebration. Some years later, in 2015, reportedly several hundreds of mostly elderly Eritreans flocked to Axum in late November for pilgrimage. Tigrayan friends and family in town hosted them, before they later returned to Eritrea. This event inspired us to undertake more focused research on people-to-people reconciliation sentiments across the border, in the shadow of the hostile and frozen bilateral relations.

As the borderlands on the Ethiopian side have been in the backwaters since 2000, neglected by the development drivers elsewhere in Tigray and Ethiopia, the people clearly want a change. The border towns and districts have slowly been dying, being depleted by their youngsters as they moved to other Ethiopian cities or migrated abroad for better opportunities. The border population has thus been eager to reconnect with its Eritrean counterparts, in order to alleviate the plight and lack of development activities induced by the closed border. Similar sentiments are believed to be harboured on the Eritrean side too. In February 2018, a small research team with colleagues from Mekelle University visited the Eritrean twin villages of Kinin and Kinto, belonging to Tsorona nus-zoba. The area is militarily controlled by Ethiopian defence forces since a 2011 border skirmish. The Eritrean villagers remained, however, and the area is now administered by the neighbouring Ethiopian woreda of Glomekeda in Adigrat zone. Life in the 'buffer zone' was full of challenges, and the villagers expressed their grievances of lack of opportunities and development as long as the border was closed. After reaching adolescence, the youth went south across the border, either to migrate to third countries or seek educational or employment opportunities in Ethiopia; since they knew that if they went north, they would end up in never-ending national service duty. Geresus (name altered), a farmer in his early 60s, explained that they are in general doing fine as their livelihood is secured with plenty of farming land available in the no-man's-land zone. He added: 'Although we do not receive any help or assistance from our local [Eritrean] authorities, Tigray administration is supplying us with all what we need in terms of social assistance and health care. And our children attend the local Tigrayan community school, as equals to their Ethiopian friends.'[10] Geresus grieved for the separation of the two peoples, and was longing for the time when the political leaders would allow the people to reconnect at the grassroots: 'If only the politicians could leave us alone, things would get back to normal quickly.'

The twin villages of Kinin and Kinto may not be representative of the broader Eritrean border population's sentiment, as the area is under military control by Ethiopia. The interest from Eritrean border villages in reconnecting with communities on the Ethiopian side does, however, manifest itself in several ways. For instance, the Ethiopian frontline commander in Zalambessa received a request in 2017 by the three neighbouring Eritrean villages to organise a joint market day for them to cross over to buy and market their produce in Zalambessa. The Ethiopian commander accepted the request, on condition that they also received a permission from Asmara to do so in order to safeguard their security when crossing the militarised zone.[11] No such permission was granted by Asmara, however.

Simultaneously, citizen reconciliation committees in Zalambessa and Senafe were working to re-establish social interaction between the two twin border towns. This was later energised by the formal peace declaration, and the grassroots lobbying group pushed for an open border. During the summer of 2018 they started to prepare for the first public reconciliation celebration in Zalambessa on 1 September. Being impatient with the sluggishness to open the border on the ground, they wanted a public event to mark the new beginning of peace rapprochement. Although supported by local authorities, the reconciliation committee in Zalambessa was a private citizen initiative. The event was sponsored by various Ethiopian business enterprises, where Eritrean and Ethiopian artists were to entertain the crowds.

Their counterparts in Senafe had organised a delegation of 300 people to join in at the festivities in Zalambessa and had received prior permission from the Eritrean force commander to cross over to the Ethiopian side. When the day occurred, however, the Eritrean delegation was denied permission to cross by the Eritrean border forces. It appeared that two days earlier the Eritrean force commander and the border unit leadership had been recalled to Asmara, and a new force commander was deployed. The formal bilateral political process between Asmara and Addis was not allowing itself to be overtaken by a grassroots-led reconciliation initiative. The power to define 'reconciliation', equal to 'enmity', was to be held by the political elites and not allowed to the grassroots. Less than two weeks later, President Isaias Afwerki and PM Abiy Ahmed were presiding over the official opening of the border on the ground, and Zalambessa was over-flooded by Eritreans who wanted to reconnect and reconcile with their Tigrayan counterparts.

---

9   Conducted around 30 November every year, the Maryam Zion festival attracts tens of thousands of pilgrims from across Ethiopia and Eritrea to Axum.

10   Interviewed February 2018.

11   Interview with the commander (name withheld), February 2018.

Declaring peace – but institutionalisation is lacking

As this is written, close to 10 months after the signing of the peace declaration in Asmara,[12] no further formal institutionalisation of the peace rapprochement has been made public. No agreement formalising cross-border traffic, trade, tariffs, immigration, etc. are ratified. Apparently, a 'road-map' for institutionalising the peace was agreed upon as late as in January this year.[13] Simultaneously, rumours were circulating that an agreement had been reached on a detailed framework regulating cross-border movement of people and goods, and that only President Isaias Afwerki's approval was pending.[14] So far, however, no concrete bilateral agreement or regulatory framework has been presented to the public, beyond the five-point peace agreement signed in Asmara in July 2018.

Ethiopian military forces are still occupying territories granted to Eritrea by the EEBC, including the symbolic village of Badme. Some redeployment of Ethiopian troops away from the border zone has been ordered, but no territories have been vacated and given back to Eritrea.[15] Likewise, Eritrea maintains full war mobilisation and has not yet announced any plans to demobilise or to reform the everlasting national service policy, quite the opposite as they are allegedly recruiting under-aged girls and boys to fill in the ranks of the service personnel deserting.[16] Neither are any plans announced for broader political and economic reforms, instituting the Eritrean Parliament and implementing the Eritrean Constitution. The country is still governed by Presidential decrees.

The formal rapprochement initiated last summer has even taken a step back, with the unexpected unilateral decision by Asmara to close the border crossings for Ethiopians to enter Eritrea in late December 2018,[17] without any official explanation given by Eritrean (or Ethiopian) authorities as to why this was imposed.[18] Only the Oumhajir-Humera crossing remained partly open for traffic, until this crossing suddenly also was closed in late April. Earlier this year, further restrictions were imposed on Eritreans wanting to cross into Ethiopia on the ground by apparently introducing a diversified policy. The Eritrean border population is allowed to cross back and forth on foot without any obstacles.[19] Eritreans from Asmara and other inland towns, however, need to apply for permission from their local authorities to travel to Ethiopia and then subsequently get an exit visa from immigration authorities in Asmara (presumably similar to an ordinary exit visa).[20] At the border, Eritrean authorities have established an immigration facility where 'inland' Eritreans need to show their exit permit and register before being allowed to cross over to Zalambessa. However, people without a permit are still crossing, but taking a one-to-two-hour detour around the formal checkpoint. If they are discovered by Eritrean border guards, they are reportedly just ordered to turn back to where they came from, without any further sanctions.[21]

The lack of institutionalising the peace declaration is obviously an increasing concern. Considering the history of outbreak of war in 1998,[22] the unpredictability of the process is glaring. As of now, the 'peace' and 'reconciliation' content of the formal agreement are concepts held hostage by the political elites in both countries, without any border-population input or influence.

Consolidating peace and reconciliation bottom-up?

Notwithstanding the hobbled formal bilateral negotiation process, the informal people-to-people reconciliation across the border on the ground is budding. People are reconnecting as individuals and families, but also as neighbouring communities, and even as local government administrators and security forces on both sides of the border. Eritreans are crossing back and forth every day, for petty trade, to buy needed commodities, to visit friends and family or to partake in religious or social ceremonies.

The opening of the border in September has, however, also radically increased the flight of Eritrean refugees, as they no longer fear being shot by the Eritrean border patrols. Latest numbers indicate that between 8,000 and 10,000 Eritreans register every month as refugees in Ethiopia. However, a sizeable group cross over and settle in Tigray or

---

12   For reasons not stated, the joint declaration was later 're-signed' in Saudi Arabia and the UAE on separate occasions. This may be inter-
      preted as giving credit to the UAE and Saudi 'support' of the process.

13   https://borkena.com/2019/01/29/eritrea-and-ethiopia-roadmap-for-cooperation-ready/

14   Interviews conducted in Mekelle and Addis Ababa in January and February 2019.

15   https://www.africanews.com/2018/08/19/ethiopia-not-withdrawing-troops-from-eritrea-front-lines-yet/

16   https://www.indepthnews.net/index.php/the-world/africa/2673-exodus-of-eritreans-in-post-peace-era-continues#.XNZzsA_eveU.twitter

17   The Ethiopian airline flights are still operating as normal, and Ethiopians are allowed to fly into Eritrea.

18   https://www.news24.com/Africa/News/eritrea-closes-border-crossings-to-ethiopian-travelers-20181228-2

19   No vehicles are allowed to drive across the border, with the exception of the Oumhajir-Humera crossing where trucks with agricultural
      produce (and possibly other goods) are reportedly intermittently allowed to cross. Transportation across the no man's land on Zalambes-
      sa and Rama crossings can be undertaken with horse-carts only. Personally observed, until mid-March 2019.

20   Interview with Eritreans in Mekelle having crossed illegally, April 2019.

21   Interview with Eritreans in Mekelle having crossed illegally, April 2019.

22   See the background causes and triggering factors to the war here: Negash, T. and Tronvoll, K. *Brothers at War: Making Sense of the Eri-
      trean-Ethiopian War* (Oxford: James Currey/Athens: Ohio University Press, 2000).

Ethiopia without registering as refugees. Elsa (name altered) is a representative of this category. I met her in the border town of Zalambessa, where she stood in the doorway of her small guesthouse and restaurant. 'All I want is to start a business and establish a future, without interference by the government', she explained.[23] Elsa left her mother and father behind in her home town of Senafe after the border between Eritrea and Ethiopia opened for free crossing in mid-September 2018. Here her small business is capitalising on the renewed cross-border traffic, as the town is experiencing an economic 'boom' as a peace dividend. When asked if she has been back to Senafe after leaving, she looked in puzzlement at me: 'Why? Whatever should I do in Senafe when the situation is as it is in Eritrea? I feel at home here in Zalambessa now.'

Local authorities in Zalambessa, as well as zonal authorities in Adigrat, confirmed that they communicate with their counterparts in Eritrea on issues of mutual concern. Likewise, both the front-line force commander and security head in Zalambessa confirmed they are talking regularly with their Eritrean counterparts, in order to 'administer' the fragile situation on the ground to the betterment of both peoples. It is doubtful, however, that this localised cross-border communication between public entities is looped through their respective capitals; this is a pragmatic approach adopted by 'statehood' on the ground, for various reasons and motivations.

For instance, in lieu of a formal bilateral agreement regulating cross-border employment and business activities, Tigray regional government has allowed all Eritreans to establish business without any license and under temporary tax exemption, in order to maintain themselves. TPLF is of the opinion that it is best for the future Eritrea that as many Eritreans as possible should stay in Tigray and the region, in order for a quick return after the situation changes in Asmara, as the dire demographic haemorrhage of the Eritrean population will constitute the key challenge to rebuilding the country.[24]

Complicating the consolidation of a sustainable people-to-people reconciliation process across the border is the increasingly politicised and polarised context in Ethiopia, where the government party EPRDF is de facto split, rendering the federal government incapacitated to implement policy on the ground in several regions of the country, and in particular in Tigray. As it seems clear that the peace rapprochement was entered into by President Isaias due to TPLF's loss of power in Addis Ababa, PM Abiy Ahmed has kept Mekelle in the dark regarding the formal bilateral process.[25] But, it is not Addis which controls the main border to Eritrea, but Mekelle. The tripartite elite power struggle between Asmara-Addis-Mekelle on defining conditions on the ground has thus the potential to hamper the people-to-people reconciliation process at the grassroots level.

Time has thus come for the political elites in both countries to allow for the people at the borderlands to reconcile and reconnect at their own device. Traditional mechanisms of reconciliation and conflict resolution will facilitate a sustainable peace bottom-up; it is just for the capitals to follow suit.

---

23   Interviewed 5 March 2019.

24   Interview with TPLF Executive Committee member, Mekelle, March 2019.

25   Interview with TPLF Executive Committee member, Mekelle, March 2019.

Dan Connell

Author, journalist and visiting scholar, African Studies Centre Boston University

Everything has changed, but nothing has changed – assessing the rapprochement between Ethiopia and Eritrea

One key indicator of the status of the relations between Eritrea and Ethiopia today and the conditions within Eritrea itself in the wake of the July 2018 peace declaration is the flow of refugees out of that country. Has it slowed since the peace agreement? No. Have refugees in Ethiopia begun to return to Eritrea? No. On the contrary, the declaration of peace and the opening of the two countries' common border triggered record outflows. I begin and end my assessment with this unsettling phenomenon.

Since 2012, I've travelled to 19 countries in Europe, North, South and Central America, Africa and the Middle East to interview Eritrean refugees on why they left their homeland, how they got out and what happened on their journeys. Most of you have heard such stories from friends and relatives. You may have a powerful one yourself, so I probably don't have to tell you how traumatic this has been for thousands of people.

But I bring it up now, because I'm convinced that it's essential to heal the deep psychological wounds that many people carry – what health professionals call PTSD (post-traumatic stress disorder) – not only to lay the groundwork for a healthy society but to build a vibrant, inclusive movement to achieve that goal. This trauma is a major obstacle to that – it cripples some people's capacity to act for change, it twists that of others into poisonous anger and it divides people from each other as effectively as religion, ethnicity or politics.

Each story is different, but they carry common threads. The majority I have interviewed, if we exclude children, fled from some form of political or religious persecution or from the **fear** of it based on something they said or did – fear being the operative feature. Most of the more than 700 refugees I've spoken with said they were convinced that nothing they could do would change things, which is both a reflection of the reality they faced and their own trauma.

Surprisingly, many said they would go back again in a minute, but only if there was genuine, deep-seated change. When I asked what that meant, they talked about getting more control over their lives and livelihoods; being able to help aging parents and afford to get married and have children; having a society of rules they could depend on, and not having to be afraid all the time. The concept of fear and uncertainty came up over and over. This is a culture where talking about one's fears, pain and grief is not easy, but doing so in a supportive context is a necessary step in getting beyond them to lead healthy lives and build a healthy society. I urge attention to this no matter what side of the political arguments you are on.

Little has changed in Eritrea since the declaration of peace last July to change any of this, which is why the outflow of refugees not only continues but accelerates. In the first month after the border opened, nearly 16,000 people registered with the UN refugee agency (UNHCR). Many were women with children who hoped to join husbands already abroad, though more than 3,000 were unmarried youths of national service age. This record outflow continued through December but briefly decreased after the two crossing points in central Tigray at Zalambessa and Rama were closed to vehicles and border guards began checking people's IDs. By February, the numbers had climbed again, however, this time with a greater share of young people, using more than a dozen mostly unmonitored crossing points. When I spoke with the head of the Ethiopian refugee agency, ARRA, in March, they were registering 300 new arrivals each day.

Assessing the current context

Nearly 10 months since peace was declared, the outlook for the future is laced with uncertainty within both countries and in the region – a jumble of promising initiatives, dangerous trends and unresolved crises. So many balls are in the air, it is difficult to know where to begin, but here's a stab at highlighting the main issues.

1.   The Eritrea-Ethiopia peace process

Though progress on the peace agreement seems to have stalled, it continues to build informally among mid-level civilian and military officials and the people on both sides of the border, and there are bilateral teams dealing with specific issues. But there are also problems and pitfalls that could derail it.

- There has been little institutionalisation at the formal level, though sources in Addis Ababa say progress is likely soon on such things as border controls, customs and port access.
- In my view, the fact there has been no move to demarcate the border yet is a good thing, as it leaves open the possibility of minor adjustments to reflect the reality on the ground once relations are normalised without derailing the process. I would expect small swaps around the Irob and Tserona areas before this is over.

- But avoiding demarcation altogether would be extremely dangerous; uncertainty itself is dangerous, given the history of the dispute and the continuing tensions. A specific timeline for demarcation is needed, whenever it is to take place. Otherwise, we're left with an *ad hoc* arrangement very like we had in the 1990s.

Here's what I worry about:

- Eritrea closed two of the four crossings to vehicular traffic in January – Rama and Zalambessa, both in central Tigray – and two more in recent weeks. There were several reasons for the first move, but the impact was to curb the petty trade with Tigray and take charge of currency exchanges, over which Eritrea had lost control.
- There's been no follow-up to the impromptu meeting at the Om Hager/Humera crossing between President Isaias Afwerki and Tigray's President Debretsion Gebremichael in January, and there is no prospect of a breakthrough in sight. This is worrisome, as Isaias has had meetings with the leaders of both the Amhara and Oromo regional states. But I do not expect progress on this until Prime Minister Abiy Ahmed makes it happen.
- Anti-*woyane* rhetoric in Eritrean official media shows no sign of letting up, and last month Isaias was reported to have told his top commanders to be on the alert for a TPLF incursion into Eritrea, as far-fetched as that sounds.
- There is a pattern here that's impossible to miss: Isaias is still fighting old battles while he pursues a broader agenda in and with Ethiopia. These trends do not bode well for a stable peace. One possibility is that he is setting up an excuse to claim national service cannot be scaled back because there is still a national security risk.

2.   The situation within Ethiopia

Despite some government claims to the contrary, inter-ethnic violence, often spontaneous, continues to erupt with devastating consequences, at the same time that organised ethnic nationalists are growing in influence, particularly in the Amhara and Oromo states:

- One of the worst recent outbreaks of inter-ethnic violence took place in the Gedeo and Guji zones of southern Ethiopia where up to 1 million people were displaced in 2018. In March, eight months after the crisis erupted, the UN reported there were still over 620,000 IDPs and enormous difficulty in gaining access to them.
- The federal government at first downplayed the conflict and only acted after international and Ethiopian media gave extensive coverage to the crisis and the State of Tigray sent Gedeo EB5m in humanitarian assistance.
- Other areas experiencing inter-ethnic violence include the Moyale region near the Kenya border, the Wollega region of western Oromiya, the southern zone of Beni-Shangul, the Harrar region between Oromiya and the Somali state, and the Qimant district of Amhara.
- Political clashes also took place recently on the outskirts of Addis between *qeeroo* militants from Oromiya and militant Addis youth over a decision by the appointed Oromo mayor to give priority for leases on newly constructed apartments to Oromos from outside the city over residents already in the queue.
- That clash put PM Abiy in a squeeze between his Oromo roots and his all-Ethiopia vision.
- Meanwhile, pan-Ethiopianist Berhanu Nega had to cancel a public forum in Bahir Dahr when Amhara youth protested his insufficiently Amhara nationalist platform.
- Both incidents highlight the rising force of ethnic nationalism. In the Amhara state this is manifested in violent conflict around Qimant and claims on two districts of Tigray – Wolkeit and Raya/Kobo – with the threat from some nationalists to go to war with Tigray.

To summarise: unrest continues in many parts of Ethiopia, while ultra-nationalist forces continue to gain strength ahead of the 2020 elections. Isaias's actions in this regard have not been designed to promote stability, especially when it comes to Tigray. And Abiy has not been putting enough time or attention into dealing with this.

3.   Regional issues

Throughout this year, Abiy's main preoccupation has been promoting peace and regional integration, focusing mainly on a three-way alliance among Eritrea, Ethiopia and Somalia.

- In March, for example, President Kenyatta of Kenya came to Addis to meet Abiy, who took him straight to Asmara for talks with Isaias on regional peace and stability.
- The next day Abiy took Isaias to Juba for talks with South Sudan officials on peace and regional security.
- Two days later Abiy hosted Somali President 'Farmajoo' and whisked him off to Nairobi for talks on Kenya-Somalia border issues; a week after that he hosted the Somaliland leader, but he was unable to get him and Farmajoo to sit down together.

- Throughout this diplomatic blitz, Isaias went along with the bilateral contacts but refused to engage with IGAD or the AU, both of which he begrudges for past acts against Eritrea; more importantly, I think, he sees them as institutions too big and too diverse to dominate until he has solidified a sub-regional base.
- In pursuit of this, he has worked with Abiy to include the extremely weak Federal Republic of Somalia in their partnership while ignoring Djibouti and Sudan.

So, what's this about?

4.   Some reflections on where this is headed

Some Eritreans interpret this as a new version of Ethiopian expansionism in which Isaias is giving Abiy control of Eritrea. I take the opposite view: regional integration is a key objective for Abiy, but the way it is unfolding reflects the long-term strategic interests of Isaias. Each may be using the other.

Building a sub-regional alliance on as shaky a foundation as these three countries provide is either the height of hubris or a crafty long-range strategy for establishing a core alliance from which to engage with stronger states and other regional bodies. My guess, based on Isaias's behaviour over the past five decades, is that it is the latter – a well-thought-out strategy. I also think that Abiy is aware of Isaias's intent but is okay with it so long as it meshes with his own vision of an integrated region whose member states eschew conflict.

Abiy's hope is that economic integration will blunt inclinations towards conflict between states by giving each one a stake in maintaining the peace. The big question is whether it will also dampen conflict **within** these states and whether it can survive as a project if it does not. Other such undertakings in Africa, the Middle East or Europe do not provide a basis for optimism. A comparable example would be the ill-fated United Arab Republic (UAR) that 'united' Egypt, the Gaza Strip and Syria, but only lasted from 1958 to 1961 when a coup in Syria caused it to collapse.

And while this is playing out, Ethiopia is in the midst of its own transition from an authoritarian, one-party state, dominated by a single ethnic group (which it has been for over a century, though the dominant groups changed), into a more open, democratic one – a state in which regional power has also shifted dramatically, even as conflict within and between regions has intensified.

Several scenarios appear possible:

a.   The continued degradation of the ruling Ethiopian Revolutionary Democratic Party, EPRDF, as a functional coalition could end with its reconfiguration into a slimmed-down party based on individual membership that replaces the 'one-region, one vote' structure it has today. This may be desirable in the long term, but it could have a destabilising impact if implemented too hastily.

- Under such conditions, the TPLF might either be excluded or could exclude itself and seek alliances with other regional parties, like the Afars, or with parties completely outside EPRDF.
- And what remains of the other two core EPRDF members, the Amhara Democratic Party (ADP) and the Oromo Democratic Party (ODP), in the face of internal challenges from ultra-nationalists in their states, might constitute the core of a slimmed-down, pan-Ethiopia EPRDF allied with elements from smaller states and pan-Ethiopia parties.

b.   EPRDF could also give way to a new formation altogether that engages in a free-for-all, after which the winners negotiate a new European-style coalition.

c.   Or, worst case, Ethiopia could fragment into competing mini-states, a number of which would face internal conflicts as well as conflicts among themselves.

d.   A fourth alternative would be for EPRDF to regain its balance in its present form, bring TPLF back into the fold (for now) and get through the 2020 elections before restructuring the political arena and with it the Constitution; that is not out of the question if the only other option is chaos.

- Bringing TPLF back into a stable, if short-term, relation with Abiy and EPRDF would provide a basis for bringing Eritrea into a dialogue with the Tigray state under the auspices of the federal government.
- It would also strengthen the federal government's capacity to address internal security issues and to pursue and consolidate other regional initiatives by engaging Tigray in the efforts, especially those involving domestic conflicts.
- This is what I think would be wisest for the short term and the best for Eritrea.

And then there is Eritrea, which has so far shown no sign of reform. This in itself is not surprising. The regime has never been quick to act, and it is clear they had not prepared for the outbreak of peace. They had no master plan when it was achieved, and they don't appear to have the human capacity to meet all the challenges and opportunities peace brings – not the diplomats, not the negotiators, not the skilled managers, not even the skilled workers to carry out the plans they will eventually come up with.

I do not see how they can avoid making some reductions in the national service and loosening the tight controls over the economy, if they want to slow the outflow of skilled manpower, let alone entice members of the diaspora with necessary skills to come back to help. Such changes are also needed to attract foreign investment and stimulate trade, and they're a precondition for curbing the flood of refugees leaving the country, which, if sustained at present levels, will eventually incapacitate the state itself and undo the gains made so far.

Against this backdrop, here are two questions I am left with:

a. Plans to improve and expand the main roads and port facilities set the stage for a major challenge to the continuation of national service as now practiced by offering a unique opportunity for transitioning to a wage-based labour force. This is a one-time opportunity. If not taken, it will not come around again. Will the government seize this chance and take the first steps toward reform?

b. What impact will the still unfolding uprising in Sudan have on the Eritrean population – and the military? It's too early to tell, but Eritrea is now bounded on two sides by countries in the midst of major transitions away from authoritarianism. Will this increase the pressure for change or cause the government to dig in its heels further and resist it?

Meanwhile, more refugees are staying in Ethiopia, due to the risks of onward migration and to the hope for change at home – and new refugee-driven initiatives are surfacing. On my last trip, I met members of an association of university students who tutor other refugees for entry exams to Ethiopian institutions and provide services to their community. This work, by design, prepares Eritreans to return home to help rebuild when circumstances and opportunity align. They at least are pointed in the right direction – home. All they need is change there and they will head back right away.

6. The rule of law and administration of justice

Bereket Habte Selassie

Scholar, legal expert and chair of the Constitutional Commission of Eritrea

Dr Bereket Habte Selassie, author of the Eritrean Constitution (Credit: Martin Plaut)

[Speech transcript by Eritrea Focus]

The rule of law

In this talk I will look at the importance of the interconnection between democracy and the rule of law will be discussed. Without democracy, the rule of law cannot stand. The two are interrelated.

What is democracy?

In my view, there are two types of democracy:

- One is what used to be called the Athenian democracy – or direct democracy – in which the Athenian people spoke in their city, directly taking care of their affairs.
- The other is representative democracy.

We have the Athenian type of democracy in Africa, including in Eritrea. There are popular meetings dealing with our affairs – it's a kind of democracy. But with the coming of Europeans and the imposition of the European system of law, and state structure, our native institutions were imposed upon.

We now have, as a result of this history, two types of democracy: direct and indirect democracy which I call representative democracy – the villagers have sent someone to the capital city, they take care of their own affairs in the village, but for national matters, which affect their lives, they have to send someone else as a representative.

This second type of democracy is what people are referring to when they talk about democracy. Nowadays, in Eritrea, having been colonised by Italy, we are, like the rest of Africa, recipients of foreign imposed laws; in our case, first Italian and then British. So, whether we like it or not, we have to deal with the challenges posed by this new type of democracy.

The doctrinal side – the equality principle

This is the fundamental notion of democracy: everyone is equal under the law, no one is above the law. This is also part of the rule of law and this is where the interconnection lies. When we talk about the rule of law, we are talking about the importance of law. The British revolutionary who became part of the American revolution (Tom Payne) said that 'in America, the law is king'.

In absolutist governments: the king is the law.

The interconnection between democracy and rule of law, and the institutions needed to support the rule of law, judges, separation of powers, and the independence of the judiciary, which are important parts of any model constitutions, are the preconditions for the existence and operation of the rule of law.

Conclusion

The rule of law, as a universally applicable principle, is an integral part of the legal and spiritual evolution of humanity. One of the achievements of the post-World War Two period has been the growth and universal acceptance of human rights under the rule of law.

Following in the footsteps of the UN Charter, numerous international resolutions and declarations have been adopted by the UN General Assembly.

A country may have a body of laws, but a body of laws without the rule of law is like a human body without a soul. The rule of law is one of the pillars of a constitutional system that provides for the protection of the civil rights and liberties of citizens. The essence of rule of law is grounded in basic human needs for certainty of rights, and protection against arbitrary power. It is, thus, conceptually opposed to the whims of capricious rulers. The rule of law creates the condition for obedience of the law, which in turn ensures peace and stability.

Mark Ellis

Executive director at the International Bar Association

Abstract

Last year's peace declaration ending two decades of conflict in Eritrea has been called a great window of opportunity for transformation. While the developments are preliminary, the peace agreement might indeed provide a chance for liberalisation, democratisation and the rule of law for the country. But how would this happen and who would bring about the change? As Executive Director of the International Bar Association, what immediately comes to my mind is constitutionalism as the foundation of state building and the role of bar associations and of the legal profession at large in bringing it about.

There are, for all of us, searing experiences that touch our lives. For me, a trip to Sarajevo in January 1995 was one of those experiences. The purpose of my visit was to meet with the six Bosnian members of the newly appointed Constitutional Court for the Federation. The Court was part of the peace agreement hammered out in the United States and was viewed as key to rebuilding a country based on the rule of law.

My task was to assist in making this Constitutional Court functional. I must admit, I thought that task was impossible. The Court was not operational. There were no procedural rules, no administrative support; the Court had never met in session and had yet to hear a case. It was an institution in name only. In order to constitute the Court, six Justices would have to meet the US experts who drafted Bosnia's new Constitution; they needed to learn of the framers' intent. It was their job to make the new Constitution a living document.

Today, when I hear the term 'rule of law' bantered about, I don't think of carefully crafted definitions or witty insights from the Washington pundits. I think back to those six justices, to the losses they suffered, to the humiliations they faced, to the dignity with which they carried themselves. I think back to what they did, as members of our profession and, most importantly, I think back to why they did it – to their unshakable belief that out of the ashes of a once civilised nation, torn apart by perverse injustice, will rise a new nation predicated on a lasting and irrevocable concept of the rule of law.

And what I realised then and there is that it is absolutely crucial that this change comes from within. Thus, it will need Eritrean lawyers and judges to rebuild the country's civil society and to act as the bedrock in recreating Eritrean constitutionalism. They must be involved with determining which options to choose and whether it would be better to have the existing draft Constitution enacted or whether to draft an entirely new one. The Eritrean legal profession must play this role. And about the legal profession, I can share a thought or two.

Introduction

Though Eritrea gained independence from Ethiopia in 1993, tensions between the two states lingered.[26] In 1998, Eritrea invaded Ethiopia which prompted the Ethiopian-Eritrean War. Some estimates suggest the war killed 100,000 people and left Eritrea with more than one-third of its territory occupied, resulting in the displacement of 650,000 people.[27] In 2000, the two nations signed the Algiers Agreement submitting to binding arbitration to resolve boundary and restitution disputes.[28] Though the Permanent Court of Arbitration awarded Eritrea the majority of the territory in dispute, the land was still mostly occupied by Ethiopia until 2017.[29] Relations were unfriendly and both societies remained closed.[30] Then Ethiopian Prime Minister Hailemariam Desalegn was unsuccessful in attempts to end the conflict.[31] He was replaced in 2018 by now-Prime Minister Abiy Ahmed. Under Prime Minister Ahmed, the Executive Committee of the ruling government announced its intentions to fully implement the 2002 arbitral ruling.[32] This surprising announcement was met with public optimism that the conflict would soon expire.[33] The government of Eritrea responded and soon the

---

26   *Eritrean, Ethiopian exchange of POWs begins*, CNN World (23 December 2000) http://edition.cnn.com/2000/WORLD/africa/12/23/eritrea.ethiopia.02/

27   *Ibid.*

28   Aglionby, J. *Ethiopia to cede land at heart of bloody conflict with Eritrea*, Financial Times (5 June 2018) https://www.ft.com/content/4d-ddc09a-68ea-11e8-8cf3-0c230fa67aec

29   *Ibid.*

30   Hennig, R.C. *Eritrea 'celebrates' 20 years of terror*, Afrol News (10 June 2013) https://web.archive.org/web/20131014134302/http://www.afrol.com/features/38272

31   *Ethiopia PM Hailemariam Desalegn in surprise resignation*, BBC News (15 February 2018) https://www.bbc.co.uk/news/world-africa-43073285

32   Maasho, A. *UPDATE 3-Ethiopia opens up telecoms, airline to private, foreign investors*, Reuters (5 June 2018) https://uk.reuters.com/article/ethiopia-privatisation/update-3-ethiopia-opens-up-telecoms-airline-to-private-foreign-investors-idUKL5N1T75Z4

33   Schemm, P. *Eritrea breaks silence and responds to Ethiopia peace overtures, will send delegation*, Washington Post (20 June 2018) https://www.washingtonpost.com/world/africa/eritrea-breaks-silence-and-responds-to-ethiopia-peace-overtures-will-send-delegation/2018/06/20/80c84c5c-745f-11e8-b4b7-308400242c2e_story.html?utm_term=.8e230d1709aa

first bilateral meeting in nearly two decades was arranged.[34]

The 2018 joint Eritrea-Ethiopia summit took place in early July 2018. The summit was between Eritrean President Isaias Afwerki, Ethiopian Prime Minister Ahmed and officials from both countries. The leaders signed a declaration formally ending the border conflict between the two states. The declaration also served to restore full diplomatic relations by including an agreement to open borders to each other for persons, goods and services.[35]

Prime Minister Ahmed has served his post since 2 April 2018.[36] He ran on a platform of promising political and economic reform and led the Ethiopian People's Revolutionary Democratic Front.[37] He is credited with ending the 20-year conflict with neighbouring Eritrea, freeing thousands of political prisoners, lifting restrictions on media and appointing women to half of all cabinet posts.[38]

Despite these advancements, more can be done. Human Rights Watch (HRW) urges the Eritrean government to issue a standing invite to UN Special Procedures, permit international NGOs access to the country and ratify the Optional Protocol on Torture, as well as the Kampala Convention and the Rome Statute.[39]

President Afwerki is the first president of Eritrea and was elected in 1993 after the Eritrean War of Independence.[40] President Afwerki led the Eritrean People's Liberation Front to victory, ending the War. Despite this feat, President Afwerki has been highly criticised by the United Nations (UN)[41] and other civil society groups[42] for human rights violations. In 2015, Reporters Without Borders ranked Eritrea last in its press freedom index.

There are reports of nascent successes of the agreement. There is hope that peace will last. People are beginning to rebuild and re-sow their lands.[43] The market in Adigrat, Ethiopia, is booming as Eritreans travel just over the border to participate.[44] The opening of borders is a stark change from previous restrictions. However, concerns around human rights violations persist. UN experts argue that Eritrea's human rights record has not changed since the agreement.[45]

Human rights in Eritrea

In June 2019, HRW issued a letter to the 41st Session of the UN Human Rights Council on Eritrea. The purpose of the letter was to '[e]nsure continued scrutiny of the human rights situation in Eritrea'.[46] Specifically, the letter denotes the continued void of free and independent press and general repression of civic space.[47] It calls on the Council to continue to scrutinise the situation in Eritrea and ensure adequate follow-up to the Special Rapporteur's report at the Council session.[48] HRW further reminds Eritrea of its obligation as a member of the Council to 'uphold the highest standards in the promotion and protection of human rights'.[49]

The year 2018 marked a significant diplomatic change for Eritrea. One month after the signing of the agreement at the Eritrea-Ethiopia summit, Eritrea and Somalia resumed diplomatic relations after 15 years without.[50] In November the same year, the UN Security Council lifted its nearly decade-long arms embargo against Eritrea.[51] Despite these less

---

34   *Ibid.*

35   *Ethiopia's Abiy and Eritrea's Afwerki declare end of war,* BBC News (9 July 2018) https://www.bbc.com/news/world-africa-44764597

36   *2019 World Press Freedom Index, Reporters Without Borders* (2019) https://rsf.org/en/ranking

37   *Ethiopia's Abiy Ahmed: The leader promising to heal a nation,* BBC News (3 January 2019) https://www.bbc.com/news/world-africa-46735703

38   *Ibid.*

39   *Ethiopia: Abiy's First Year as Prime Minister, Review of Commitments to International Human Rights Norms, Human Rights Watch* (6 April 2019) https://www.hrw.org/news/2019/04/06/ethiopia-abiys-first-year-prime-minister-review-commitments-international-human

40   *Eritrea profile – Leaders,* BBC News (1 May 2014) https://www.bbc.co.uk/news/world-africa-13349076

41   Cumming-Bruce, N. *Torture and Other Rights Abuses Are Widespread in Eritrea, U.N. Panel Says, The New York Times* (8 June 2015) https://www.nytimes.com/2015/06/09/world/africa/eritrea-human-rights-abuses-afwerki-un-probe-crimes-against-humanity-committed.html?_r=0

42   *Eritrea: Rampant repression 20 years after independence, Amnesty International* (9 May 2013) https://www.amnesty.org/en/latest/news/2013/05/eritrea-rampant-repression-years-after-independence/

43   Peralta, E. *'Peace Is Everything': Ethiopia And Eritrea Embrace Open Border After Long Conflict, NPR* (4 December 2018) https://www.npr.org/2018/12/04/671260821/peace-is-everything-ethiopia-and-eritrea-embrace-open-border-after-long-conflict?t=1560345945550

44   *Ethiopia-Eritrea border boom as peace takes hold, BBC News* (9 January 2019) https://www.bbc.co.uk/news/world-africa-46794296

45   Schlein, L. *UN: No Rights Progress in Eritrea After Peace Deal With Ethiopia,* VOA News (16 March 2019) https://www.voanews.com/africa/un-no-rights-progress-eritrea-after-peace-deal-ethiopia

46   *Letter to 41st Session of the UN Human Rights Council on Eritrea,* Human Rights Watch (11 June 2019) https://www.hrw.org/news/2019/06/12/letter-41st-session-un-human-rights-council-eritrea

47   *Ibid.*

48   *Ibid.*

49   *Ibid.*

50   *Eritrea: Events of 2018,* Human Rights Watch (9 November 2018) https://www.hrw.org/world-report/2019/country-chapters/eritrea

51   *Ibid.*

restrictive conditions, by the end of the year there was no sign of Eritrea ending its repression of basic rights.[52]

Prior to the agreement, President Afwerki used the conflict with Ethiopia to justify authoritarianism. Practices at the time included: forced enrolment into national service without service limits, jailing journalists and other opponents without trial, and prohibiting independent media and political parties and NGOs.[53] President Afwerki also prohibited elections, arguing it would weaken the state's defenses.[54] Though implementation of a constitution was approved by a constituent assembly in 1997, President Afwerki deferred it indefinitely, claiming it a strategy in response to the war.[55] Just two weeks before the agreement with Ethiopia was reached, the UN Human Rights Council bemoaned President Afwerki's 'systematic, widespread and gross human rights violations'.[56]

Despite the agreement, by the end of 2018 conditions had not changed.[57] The UN condemned the armed forces of the nation,[58] the Office of National Security, the police, the Information Ministry, the Ministry of Justice and the People's Front for Democracy and Justice – the only party in power since the country gained independence in 1993.[59]

In 2018, a UN Special Rapporteur reported that human rights violations 'continue unabated'.[60] Some of the denoted persisting human rights violations include:

- repression in armed forces;
- systematic forced labour;
- detention of those who criticise army practices;
- more restrictions on religious practice;
- attempts to report violence suffered by women to the army and police refused;
- torture and ill-treatment inflicted on people during military training and in the army;
- harsh punishment of desertion from the army;
- extrajudicial execution of soldiers for cowardice in the context of war with Ethiopia;
- extrajudicial execution of conscripts during peacetime;
- shoot-to-kill policy to prevent people fleeing the country.[61]

HRW criticised the government for using the high school system to forcibly conscribe young people into national service. This severely impacts the right to education and, over time, has eroded people's motivations and educational qualifications.[62] While the practices surrounding the service constitute human rights violations, Eritrea is also criticised for committing human rights violations during this forced national service.[63] Service members are often given insufficient food, water, hygienic services and medical care.[64] Regardless of gender, all Eritreans have a duty to participate in the national service.[65] This requirement does not shield women from particular discriminations in service. Women are at a disproportionate risk of sexual violence, so much so that the Human Rights Council states 'the commission finds that... it is to such a degree it also constitutes sexual slavery and torture'.[66] Many suffer irreparable psychological damage, especially women and victims of sexual violence.

Women outside of service also face a number of human rights violations. Women victims of sexual violence and other abuse have no way of seeking protection from the state as it is the very state that is responsible for the perpetration of such crimes. Recorded testimonies highlight the limited and ineffective legal systems that are in place.[67] There is a deficiency of prosecution of, protection from and punishment for these crimes.[68]

52   Ibid.
53   Ibid.
54   Ibid.
55   Ibid.
56   Ibid.
57   Ibid.
58   G.A. Res. 35/35 (6 July 2017) https://documents-dds-ny.un.org/doc/UNDOC/GEN/G17/183/98/PDF/G1718398.pdf?OpenElement
59   Ibid.
60   UN Human Rights Council *Report of the detailed findings of the Commission of Inquiry on Human Rights in Eritrea*, U.N. Doc. A/HRC/29/CRP.1 (5 June 2015) https://www.ohchr.org/Documents/HRBodies/HRCouncil/ColEritrea/A_HRC_29_CRP-1.pdf
61   Ibid.
62   Ibid.
63   Ibid.
64   Ibid. at 337.
65   Ibid. at 340.
66   Ibid. at 379.
67   Ibid. at 188.
68   Ibid.

Additionally, the government has created a pervasive net of espionage, control and repression within the country.[69] President Afwerki and his government have created complex and multi-layered systems conducting surveillance on Eritreans.[70] Everyone is a target, especially people trying to flee, members of certain religious groups and NGOs, critics of the government, the detained, and individuals suspected of spying for foreign agents.[71] Government spies are everywhere, including outside of Eritrea to control Eritrean diaspora.[72] While some government spies are recruited by the government, there is also a public expectation that everyone spies on their neighbours.[73]

The level of surveillance and control resembles the draconian measures taken in the past to contain epidemics, as Eritrean nationals are being forced to prove their obedience to the regime.[74] The government keeps a database of all family units and members. All citizens living in the country are required to maintain good standing to access the most basic necessities.[75] Buying bread, for example, requires each citizen to prove his or her good standing. Only with this condition can the person receive a daily coupon for fulfilling basic needs. Moreover, each member of a household must prove the same in order to receive coupons. The absence of a family member results in the withdrawal of coupons from the family or unit.

The system was originally implemented in the capital city, Asmara, but is reportedly spreading throughout the country. The same coupon system is also used when accessing other utilities. The system is used when registering children in school, renewing passports and acquiring licenses or visas.[76] The system is 'aimed at controlling people'.[77] In practice, no citizen is free to move within the country and across the borders; this is part of the government's alleged objective to protect the country's safety and public order. Consequently, migration is a crime.

Eritrea did not have an 'Eritrean spring'. Instead, there was a return to political elites when building Eritrea's independence. There was a crackdown around politics and the exercise of all fundamental freedoms.[78] All opposition newspapers were closed and a campaign of arrests was underway that was directed towards those who criticised the totalitarian behavior of the regime.[79] While only one TV station, newspaper and radio station survived, the Constitution was wholly suspended and the entire Parliament was disbanded. The government relied on the justification that there was a state of emergency due to the conflict with Ethiopia.

The campaign targeted government opponents. They are constantly subjected to arbitrary arrests, illegal detentions, torture, enforced disappearances, and also to extra-judiciary executions.[80] Living under inhuman and degrading conditions, detainees are subjected to torture, mistreatment and violence.[81] While there is no differential treatment between detainees and prisoners, most of the persons held in detention are not convicts.[82] All held are subject to forced prison labour and are not compensated for their work.[83] The labour is often heavy manual labour and unskilled work carried out under extreme conditions. In effect, it is a form of punishment and has severe consequences for the mental and physical health of people.[84] Notably, hungry detainees are forced to work and harvest vegetables and are severely punished if they attempt to eat the produce.[85] There are some reports that detainees have died as a result of the labour conditions, poor sanitary conditions and ill-treatment.[86]

When looking at actions towards building democracy in the country, it is clear that all attempts have so far failed.

---

69   *See generally,* at *supra* note 36.

70   *Ibid.* at 91.

71   *Ibid.*

72   *Ibid.*

73   *Ibid.*

74   *See generally,* at *supra* note 36.

75   *Ibid.*

76   *Ibid.*

77   *Ibid.* at 97.

78   *Ibid.* at 121.

79   *See generally,* at *supra* note 36.

80   *Ibid.* at 134.

81   *See generally,* at *supra* note 36.

82   *Ibid.* at 441.

83   *Ibid.*

84   *Ibid.* at 445.

85   *Ibid.* at 446.

86   *Ibid.*

The legal profession in Eritrea and the role of international law

The reality of the legal profession in Eritrea could not be further from the aspirational goal. The nearly two-decades of authoritarian rule has forced nearly one-third of the country's population to flee.[87] Included among the fleeing emigrants are almost all the legal professionals. Even after fleeing, Eritrean lawyers cannot practice their profession because the government continues to create blockades. The government routinely refuses to release academic credentials and any certifications, without which finding employment is practically impossible.[88]

Legal education has a relatively short history of existence in Eritrea. The University of Asmara, Eritrea's only university, started to provide legal education post-independence in 1992.[89] Specifically, the university established a law programme in 2003. Despite technically operating from 2003 to 2009, the law department did not admit new students after 2006.[90] In addition to the lack of institutions teaching law, the publication of new major codes since 2006 requires a complete restructuring of legal education. As it existed, the university taught law with legal commentaries, casebooks and other materials, mostly published in the 1960s.[91]

Statutory bodies involved in the licensing of lawyers and the regulation of the profession are foreseen in Eritrean law, specifically in the Advocates Proclamation (Proclamation) of 1996.[92] The Proclamation regulates admission, professional responsibility and disciplinary matters of advocates.[93] However, the government has consistently prohibited the establishment of these bodies, which include the Legal Committee of the Ministry of Justices (MOJ), as well as the Association of Advocates (Bar Association). Today, the MOJ has simply ignored applications for admission as an advocate.[94] With the exception of those already practicing law (who got their licenses soon after the entry into force of the Advocates Proclamation in 1996), the MOJ has simply ignored applications for admission as an advocate.

The Eritrean Law Society (ELS)

As we know, the legal profession has witnessed some revival in the Eritrean diaspora. In 2003, many law graduates that had fled the country established the Eritrean Law Society (ELS) as a non-profit organisation in Virginia, United States. The ELS is the only professional association of Eritrean lawyers. Free and independent professional associations are not allowed to be established in Eritrea, therefore the ELS was founded and currently operates outside the state.[95]

The ELS aims at promoting the Eritrean legal system, providing legal services to Eritrean citizens and increasing public understanding of the rule of law and democratic principles.[96] The ELS also operates to lobby governments, organisations and individuals to pay attention to 'gross human rights violations against Eritreans'.[97] This is a crucial underpinning to the investigation, monitoring, recording and publishing of human rights violations against Eritreans both inside and out of the state.[98]

The ELS might be somewhat removed from performing the usual functions of a traditional bar association. However, it will be a crucial agent of change when it comes to reviving democracy and rule of law in Eritrea. And if a window of opportunity truly opens, rebuilding the legal institutions will be instrumental in the revitalisation and reconstruction of civil society.

Membership of the ELS is open to all interested persons in the legal field who are committed to achieving the flagship objectives of the organisation.[99]

The role of bar associations in general

'I have come to firmly believe that bar associations equip lawyers, to equip society, with the laws, tools and institutions to promote and defend the principles of the rule of law. The legal profession has the crucial

87   Weldehaimanot, S.M. 'The Undermined Law Society and Legal Profession in Eritrea' (2012) X(2) International Journal of Civil Society Law
        https://ssrn.com/abstract=2066144

88   Ibid.

89   Dirar, L. and Teweldebirhan, K.T UPDATE: Introduction to Eritrean Legal Systems and Research, Hauser Global Law School Program (2015)
        https://www.nyulawglobal.org/globalex/Eritrea1.html#LawyersandLegalProfession

90   Ibid.

91   Ibid.

92   Ibid.

93   Ibid.

94   Ibid.

95   Eritrean Law Society (ELS) http://erilaw.org/about-us/

96   Ibid.

97   Ibid.

98   Ibid.

99   Ibid.

role of "raising the alarm" and alert the wider community if laws, which would not otherwise be subject to scrutiny, are operating inefficiently or unfairly.'[100]

Bar associations have a responsibility to constantly advocate change in the law to enhance the welfare of society. Bar associations are uniquely situated to do this. Given the nature of their work and the frequency and proximity with which they observe the law in action, the legal profession is often in a prime position to closely monitor and, in turn, shape the development of law.[101]

Bar associations:

- regulate the profession;
- strengthen the role of lawyers; and
- safeguard their independence.

These responsibilities are based on Article 19 of the International Covenant on Civil and Political Rights (ICCPR) and the UN Basic Principles on the Role of Lawyers.[102]

lawyers must be allowed to carry out their work 'without intimidation, hindrance, harassment or improper interference.'[103]

The UN Basic Principles also:

- require governments and professional associations of lawyers to ensure that lawyers can enter the profession and continue to practice without discrimination, including on the grounds of political or other opinions;
- require governments and professional associations to ensure that lawyers can exercise their profession without intimidation or improper interference.[104]

For bar associations to be relevant to society, they must promote the rule of law and access to justice.

Here, 'rule of law' is meant in its broadest sense. The functional definition most commonly used for rule of law may be found in the principles first attributed to Plato and articulated by the English jurist Albert Dicey in his seminal work, *An Introduction to the Study of the Law of the Constitution*. He articulated the elements to be:

- the supremacy of law over arbitrary power;
- equality of all before the law;
- the law of the constitution as a consequence of individual rights enforced by the courts.[105]

In Prague in 2005, the International Bar Association's (IBA) Council passed a Rule of Law Resolution, reiterating the fundamental principles of what we understand the rule of law to mean:

- an independent, impartial judiciary;
- the presumption of innocence;
- the right to a fair and public trial without undue delay;
- a rational and proportionate approach to punishment;
- a strong and independent legal profession;
- strict protection of confidential communications between lawyer and client;
- equality of all before the law.[106]

Most importantly, bar associations must take an active interest in the promotion and advancement of the legal rights of individuals, including human rights.

100   Dr Mark S. Ellis, Executive Director of the International Bar Association, London, United Kingdom.

101   Kerimbaev, A. et al. *The Role of Bar Associations in Successful Legal Profession Development in Transitioning Countries (Program)*, Fordham School of Law https://www.fordham.edu/info/25022/regulation_of_the_legal_profession_and_judiciary/8113/the_role_of_bar_associa-tions_in_successful_legal_profession_development_in_transitioning_countries_program

102   International Covenant on Civil and Political Rights, UN Human Rights Office of the High Commissioner, 23 March 1976 https://www.ohchr.org/en/professionalinterest/pages/ccpr.aspx (the ICCPR is viewed as customary international law in its main provisions and, thus, all countries must abide by these principles).

103   These principles affirm the right of lawyers to freedom of expression, including 'the right to take part in public discussion of matters concerning the law, the administration of justice and the promotion and protection of human rights', and provide that *Ibid*.

104   Basic Principles on the Role of Lawyers, UN Human Rights Office of the High Commissioner, 7 September 1990 https://www.ohchr.org/en/professionalinterest/pages/roleoflawyers.aspx

105   Dicey, A. *An Introduction to the Study of the Law of the Constitution*.

106   *IBA Annual Conference, Prague, 2005* https://www.ibanet.org/Education_and_Internships/conference_reports_prague.aspx

Bar associations in Eritrea

While Proclamation 88/96 and other domestic laws do not prohibit or ban the formation of an independent bar association in Eritrea, today, none exist.[107] Admission to the bar, and concurring bar status review, is the sole responsibility of the Legal Committee of the MOJ. The Committee has not issued a new license in years and the number of lawyers in private practice is dwindling due to old age, health and the like.[108] In practice, getting a license, and keeping that license, to practice law means professionals have to go through a long list of bureaucratic conditions and confirm unwavering national support.[109]

International law in Eritrea

With the exception of the suspended 1997 Constitution, there is no law or policy clarifying the status or mechanics of turning international law into domestic law or transferring it into the Eritrean legal system.[110] Despite being a signatory to a number of international conventions, the current status of international or customary law as a source of law in Eritrea is unclear. Courts do not cite rules of international or customary law. Moreover, advocates do not base their arguments on the same. While a few pieces – mainly those related to loans and regional economic zones – of Eritrean legislation domesticate international agreements, these proclamations do not contain language intending to give effect to international agreements.[111]

Additionally, there is no domestic law translating private international law. The Civil Procedure Code, does, however, contain a few articles on the enforcement and execution of foreign made judgments.[112]

Constitutional drafting and structure

But how can the rule of law be brought about once the dictatorship has been removed? Should the Constitution – drawn up and agreed on, but never enacted – be used as the basis for a new order? Or should it be a temporary 'fix' until wider consultations can be held? It will be vitally important to agree on the priority of events. This will have to include the lifting of repression; freedom of expression, assembly and organisation and the holding of free and fair elections. How can this be achieved while maintaining peace and security in a troubled region?

In 1994, the transitional government established a Constitutional Commission. The Commission was charged with drafting a constitution to be ratified by a Constituent Assembly. The Commission submitted a draft Constitution to the Assembly in 1997. The drafted Constitution establishes a unitary state and ensures any government is formed in accord with democratic procedures. The Constitution also establishes and outlines the three branches of the government: the legislature, judiciary and executive.[113] It also accounts for four constitutional bodies: an Auditor General, a National Bank, a Civil Service Administration and an Electoral Commission.[114] Moreover, the draft Constitution provides a section on fundamental rights and freedoms. This section incorporates the majority of the rights and duties adopted in the International Bill of Rights.[115] The Assembly ratified the Constitution in 1997, however, it has yet to come into effect.[116]

It should be noted that the 2015 Codes of Civil and Criminal Procedure make reference to a constitution. However, as presented, it is unclear whether the references are to the 1997 Constitution or one prior.[117] For example, Article 362 of the Code of Civil Procedure says the Supreme Court may grant an appeal by any party to any case that supposes an issue of constitutionality of a law. The Code of Criminal Procedure also empowers any person to petition any court for release if the detention violates the laws and Constitution.[118] Despite these express references, courts in Eritrea hardly rely on provisions of the Constitution.

Furthermore, the present structure of the government does not fit with the democratic one envisaged by the Constitution.[119] The structure of the state, as proscribed by the Constitution, delineates: separation of powers; a National Assembly composed of representatives elected by all Eritrean citizens aged 18 and over; that the National

---

107   Dirar and Teweldebirhan, *supra* note 65.
108   *Ibid.*
109   *Ibid.*
110   *Ibid.*
111   *Ibid.*
112   *Ibid.*
113   *Ibid.*
114   *Ibid.*
115   *Ibid.*
116   *Ibid.*
117   *Ibid.*
118   *Ibid.*
119   *Supra* note 36 at 69.

Assembly would elect the president, and in the alternative, could impeach a president; and that both the President and the National Assembly serve elected terms of five years, with a two-term limit on the President.[120]

Paradoxically, the government is led by the Eritrean People's Liberation Front (EPLF), invested with forming a transitional political structure until the establishment of a constitutional government in Eritrea, which was never created.[121] The executive branch, the Council of the Government of Eritrea, later named Cabinet, is made of EPLF members only. The Constitution, which was supposed to transition the political landscape into a constitutional system through domestic political processes, has been set aside and political power has ever since been with the central government of Eritrea.[122] After gaining independence, a National Assembly was created, as a unicameral structure with the power to issue laws, prepare and approve domestic and foreign policies, ratify international agreements, approve national budget and development plans and establish ministries and other governmental agencies.[123] However, the National Assembly has not led to any effective legislation concerning law making processes in Eritrea. It has been completely absent from the Eritrean political landscape since 2001.[124]

One of the most notable safeguards guaranteed in the Constitution that is missing from current Eritrean practices is national elections. When confronted with the lack of democratic elections in 2014, the government retorted that national elections will be held once the threats to national security and sovereignty are eliminated.[125]

Commentary on constitutional experience

'My own experience with constitutional drafting occurred after the fall of the Berlin Wall 1989. The newly emerging countries of the former Eastern Europe were focused foremost on constitutional drafting. The ABA CEELI project, which I directed, was inundated with requests for assistance in constitutional drafting.'[126]

CEELI, the Central and East Europe Law Initiative, which was founded in 1999, is an independent, non-profit, non-governmental organisation dedicated to advancing the rule of law across various countries.[127] CEELI was promulgated on protecting fundamental rights and individual liberties, promoting transparent, incorruptible, accountable governments, supporting economic development and growth and encouraging peaceful resolutions of disputes.[128] Immediately after the fall of the Berlin Wall, countries in the former Eastern Europe contacted CEELI overnight with requests for assistance in constitutional drafting.

The challenge to the requests was determining what exact procedure should be used. Some suggested simply creating a *pre-written* constitution with:

The Draft of _____ country [Fill in the blank with each country].

However, the ABA CEELI project took a different approach:

- CEELI would not draft the constitution; national drafting committees would be required to do so.
- CEELI created teams of constitutional experts who would act as a collective sounding board to the drafting committees, and comment on critical issues in the proposed draft.
- The CEELI teams would include non-US legal experts to ensure diversity of opinion.

CEELI took a backseat role in aiding states developing constitutions to ensure the true origins of the country's constitution. The CEELI team would comment on critical issues, such as the independence of the judiciary and separation of powers, but would otherwise remain a sounding board. Despite being thought of as a temporary institution (the State Department and USAID thought CEELI and its mission would last for one, two, maybe three years) still operates today as part ABA ROLI (Rule of Law Initiative) and aids in promoting the rule of law throughout the entire world.

ROLI remains an influential institution today in promoting the importance of judicial independence which furthers the rule of law. Moreover, ROLI is committed to addressing the role of the judiciary and its relation to other state powers in modern democracies. Eritrea currently has no judiciary, let alone an impartial or independent one, which is fundamental to a successful and long-standing democracy.

---

120   *Ibid.* at 71.

121   *See generally,* at *supra* note 36.

122   *Ibid.*

123   *Ibid.*

124   *Ibid.*

125   *Ibid.*

126   Dr Mark S. Ellis, Executive Director of the International Bar Association, London, United Kingdom.

127   *Mission of the CEELI Institute,* CEELI Institute Prague https://ceeliinstitute.org/who-we-are/mission/

128   *Ibid.*

The judiciary

To safeguard the separation of powers, the 1997 Constitution provides for a Judicial Committee to be charged with appointing judges. However, this Committee has not been created so judges are appointed, reassigned and dismissed at the will of the President.[129] The independence of the judiciary is quasi-non-existent and routinely violated by an executive-dominated government.[130] While a few remaining judges were trained at the Law Faculty in Asmara, most are previous military officers.[131] The officers are without specific legal training or have been recruited to the post through their national service. Their careers are managed by the MOJ and the Ministry of Defense (MOD).[132]

As far as the judiciary is concerned, its structure follows the structure of the local government. Material jurisdiction of courts depends on the amount of money involved in the case. There are four levels of jurisdiction: Community Courts, Zoba Courts, the High Court and the Supreme Court as a court of last resort.[133] Moreover, courts can be divided into three categories: Civil, Military and Special Courts.[134]

However, an independent and effective judiciary is necessary, ensuring laws are certain and not used arbitrarily to the detriment of citizens. Such a judiciary must be founded on strong institutional bases and bound to accepted legal principles. The reality is that most African countries, indeed, most developing countries worldwide, struggle with the maintenance of an independent judiciary in some form or another.

Accountability and reporting

One crucial issue that must be faced is the challenge between peace and accountability in post-conflict environments like Eritrea. Violations committed during the conflict should be acknowledged and recognised. Those who have committed gross violations of international humanitarian and human rights law should be brought to justice. The government of Eritrea is no longer the only player in the justice arena.

There was a time when states were the only relevant actors within international law. Given distinctions of politics, culture, religion and history, and the uncompromising nature of state sovereignty, it was impossible to apply a uniform set of rules at the international level, except as a matter of state action and diplomatic effort. However, over the last half century there has been a shift away from the accepted doctrine that international law was the exclusive domain of the sovereign state.[135] Today, the interpretation of international law has expanded to include and recognise new actors as entities of legitimate concern. Nowhere has this been more relevant than in the sphere of international criminal and human rights law, where the preeminent focus is on the individual, even with the borders of sovereign states.

Modern international law now extends beyond the regulation of inter-state conduct, and into regulation of the conduct between the state and the individual. A new doctrine – that individual human rights might, under certain conditions, take precedence over state sovereignty – changed the international legal order forever.

And with this new doctrine has come recognition that governments' power to grant impunity for these crimes should be limited. Of course, the relationship between demands for accountability and the interest of the state is not always harmonious, and can lead to complexities, contradictions and occasional collisions of justice and government processes. However, states now find themselves restricted by the emerging frameworks and mechanisms of international humanitarian law. The parameters for bartering peace against justice have tightened. Impunity no longer has a place in the diplomatic toolbox. This should hold true for Eritrea as well.

The International Bar Association (IBA)

The International Bar Association (IBA) stands ready to assist Eritrea, and its legal profession, in efforts to create a constitutional democracy in Eritrea, based on the rule of law and the protection of human rights.

The IBA – the global voice of the legal profession – is the foremost organisation for international legal practitioners, bar associations and law societies. Established in 1947, shortly after the creation of the **United Nations,** it was born out of the conviction that an organisation made up of the world's bar associations could contribute to global stability and peace through the administration of justice.

In the ensuing 70 years since its creation, the organisation has evolved from an association comprised exclusively

129   See generally, at supra note 36.
130   Ibid.
131   Ibid.
132   Ibid.
133   Dirar and Teweldebirhan, supra note 65.
134   Ibid.
135   See Ellis, M.S. Combating Impunity and Enforcing Accountability as a Way to Promote Peace and Stability – The Role of International War Crimes Tribunals (Cambridge: Cambridge Scholars Publishing, 2014).

of bar associations and law societies to one that incorporates individual international lawyers and entire law firms. The present membership is comprised of more than 80,000 individual international lawyers from most of the world's leading law firms and some 190 bar associations and law societies spanning more than 170 countries.

The IBA has considerable expertise in providing assistance to the global legal community, and through its global membership, it influences the development of international law reform and helps to shape the future of the legal profession throughout the world.

7. The national economy in an integrating region

David Styan

Lecturer, International Relations, Birkbeck College, University of London

Eritrea's economy; domestic constraints and regional integration

Introduction

These notes highlight selected issues of relevance to the Eritrean economy's current and future position in the region. They are schematic, being designed primarily to provide a framework for debate. The text is structured in three sections: the first briefly reviews the fragmentary state of knowledge about Eritrea's current economic status in the region. There has been an almost total absence of economic data in recent decades. Without this, conventional comparative economic analyses of potential policy changes, trends of trade or investment flows, or the constraints of regional integration are necessarily speculative.

Rather more surprisingly, there is also a total silence from the current government regarding its assessment of the radically changed regional economic outlook since mid-2018. There is no clarity as to its revised economic policies and objectives towards Ethiopia. It is silent about how it conceives the economic content of 'peace'. Uncertainties including the nature and scale of potential investment in infrastructure; particularly from the formal sponsors of Ethio-Eritrean rapprochement, Saudi Arabia and the United Arab Emirates. A broader consideration is whether the Eritrean government's extensive series of diplomatic overtures to both Arab and IGAD states will produce any tangible change to Eritrea's economic policies and outlook, such as improved trade ties or access for economic migrants.

The second section highlights a series of underlying economic realities and constraints. It emphasises that near identical constraints face both the current administration in Asmara, and any subsequent reformed or replacement authorities. Most of the current structural economic constraints will remain, irrespective of what kind of constitutionally-based 'transition' or 'reformist' government Eritrean activists may aspire to. Key constraints include both the formal sector's continued reliance on extractive industries as a source of growth, and the lack of employment opportunities.

It is worth stressing at the outset that such constraints are hardly unique in post-colonial Africa; Eritreans considering their economic future would do well to avoid essentialism; they shouldn't see their own predicament as unique. Yes, Eritrea has an unusually convoluted history; and Eritrea's economic future will also remain inextricably bound-up in that of Ethiopia. Yet being overshadowed by a large neighbour's economy is hardly unusual and it also shares many economic characteristics, both with other small African states and countries which have suffered acute mismanagement and authoritarianism post-liberation. Eritreans would do well to learn from others' mistakes. The reality is that – even under an optimistic scenario of a peaceful transition – the post-Isaias economic policy dilemmas facing both the public and private sectors will not be dramatically different from those facing the current PFDJ executive in the short-run.

In the longer-run, there are at least three critical policy choices facing any new administration. First, what role is envisaged for the private sector? This is closely linked to the second choice; what economic role is envisaged for Eritreans abroad? The diaspora will clearly remain the primary source of foreign exchange, as at present. What might change, given the right policy incentives, is the potential for inward remittance-funded investments. The third choice is to what extent a new administration will have enhanced potential for mobilising new multi- and bi-lateral funds, most particularly for infrastructure development?

The third section finally briefly examines three spheres influencing Eritrea's potential regional economic relations. These are: (i) the consolidation and reconfiguration of economic ties with Ethiopia; (ii) the impetus generated by the new commitment of all of the states in the Intergovernmental Authority on Development (the Horn's regional inter-state body, IGAD) to enhancing regional integration in the Horn of Africa since 2018 (the key by-product of Ethio-Eritrean rapprochement); (iii) broader regional and international dynamics involving external powers.

The latter include the spill-over into the Horn of broader Middle Eastern strategic realignments. Most notably those triggered by the Gulf Cooperation Council (GCC) splits between the Saudi bloc and Qatar, the Yemen war and Turkey's growing influence in the Horn. There is a separate dynamic created by the rapid emergence of China as a significant economic actor in the Red Sea region.

1.

1.1 The 'known unknowns': Eritrea's absent economic and trade data

Standard international economic data reporting has been sparse and fragmentary since 1998. This is normally aggregated and published by multilateral agencies, who derive it from nationally generated statistics. Thus, data from the World Bank, International Monetary Fund and its International Financial Statistics (IFS) series are almost entirely lacking. Nor is separate national information on international trade, balance of payments or remittance flows available. While the Central Bank and monetary authorities must collect data to inform day-to-day currency and fiscal management, notably on forex and remittances, this is not published or available externally.

A preliminary sign of possible change came in mid-May 2019, when an IMF team visited Asmara for a regular Article IV Consultation with Eritrea. This was the first such discussion in 10 years. The team's report noted that 'The information base of economic developments in Eritrea has deteriorated, and the conditions prevailing in the country have given rise to data and capacity constraints.' It added that 'In recent years, policies have tried to adapt to the difficult conditions prevailing in the country.' A sustained period of high fiscal deficits – reversed over the past three years – has led to a heavy public debt burden, the banking sector is vulnerable and foreign exchange is scarce. The Fund noted 'existing restrictions on economic activity', but few other details emerged from the short press statement, although the visit may lead to the provision of technical assistance on data and policy.

A partial exception to absent data appears to be the African Development Bank's 'African Economic Outlook'. Its 2019 version appears the only conventional source providing some estimates of economic activity. However, it is unclear from where the ADB draws their data and interpretation. They recently claimed, with somewhat implausible precision: 'The current account surplus declined from 0.7% of GDP in 2017 to an estimated 0.3% in 2018 as the economy continued to face fluctuating commodity prices for its traditional exports – gold and copper. Gross foreign reserves continued to improve, increasing from 5.1 months of imports in 2017 to 7.3 months in 2018 due to increased mining sector revenue.' No data is given for regional trade trends, or the balance of payments overall.

More relevantly to our concerns here, the ADB go on to note: 'Institutional weaknesses include […] a lack of reliable statistics to guide planning, decision making, program implementation, and monitoring and evaluation.' If balance of payments data exist, they are not accessible to Eritrean citizens. Nor are government accounts of taxes levied on foreign trade or FDI published. As such, data on regional economic interactions tends to be derived from partners' trade reports – themselves invariably very partial – or piecemeal reports by recent investors.

1.2 We know even less about how Eritrea's government perceives the regional 'peace dividend'

In terms of the recently changed outlook for Eritrea's economic policy and regional economic stance since mid-2018, schematically we can distinguish between: (a) what has been vaguely suggested, and (b) what has actually happened.

On Sunday 3 March 2019 Eritrea's President Isaias Afwerki received Ethiopia's Prime Minister Abiy Ahmed, and Kenyan President Uhuru Kenyatta in Asmara. The trio had also just visited Juba in neighbouring Southern Sudan. This was just the latest in what has become a diplomatic whirlwind of such regional inter-governmental meetings since Ethio-Eritrean rapprochement was signed last July. The series of such bi- and multi-lateral inter-ministerial meetings included several high-profile trips by Isaias to Ethiopia.

Yet, nine months on, Asmara has still published no detailed plans as to what changes, if any, it intends to make to its autarkic economic development strategies, what its economic policy objectives are in the protracted negotiations with Ethiopia or what opportunities it hopes the lifting of UN sanctions will offer its economy.

On 22 February, two weeks before the Ethio-Eritrean-Kenyan summits in Juba and Asmara, Ethiopia's then Foreign Minister Workneh Gebeyehu and his Eritrean counterpart Osman Saleh met for their fourth 'ministerial consultation'. However, the 'High-level Joint Commission' proposed in the September 2018 Jeddah Agreement signed by the two countries has yet to emerge, despite the fact that documents covering 'port utilization, transport, trade and customs' exist in draft form; Ethiopia's Ministry of Trade and Industry announced in late May 2019 that they had sent two cross-border trade agreements to Asmara for approval.

In the economic domain, the seven-point Jeddah Agreement is aspirational but nebulous:

(Article Two) The two countries will promote comprehensive cooperation in the political, security, defence, economic, trade, investment, cultural and social fields on the basis of complementarity and synergy.

(Article Three) The two countries will develop Joint Investment Projects, including the establishment of Joint Special Economic Zones.

However, clearly there have been substantive short-term changes in the Eritrean economy triggered by the opening of borders with Ethiopia and the reestablishment of flights between Asmara and Addis in July 2018. The supply of foodstuffs, consumer goods and accompanying reduction of shortages and inflationary pressures in Eritrea are the most obvious, prompting significant swings in Birr-Nakfa exchange rates.

The analysis of these is beyond our scope, but clearly the observable trends in cross-border trade are not the result of planned changes or developmental strategies by the authorities in Asmara. In particular, there seems little sense of how Eritrean para-statal or private capital is expected to participate in the new wholesale and retail flows.

2. Existing economic realities and constraints

Potential regional economic integration needs to be assessed in the context of at least three areas of constraints: the mining sector, infrastructure and employment policies.

2.1 Eritrea's formal economy's continued reliance on mining as a source of growth

While there appears to have been a modest expansion in real estate and construction in recent years, particularly in Asmara, most analysts, and the Eritrean government itself, stress the role that foreign mining has had upon overall economic growth. Existing mines, and future prospecting and development, are likely to remain key components of Eritrea's economy, including as sources of foreign exchange (via both inward FDI and export earnings).

The details of Bishaa (Nevsum/Zijin) gold mine project and its evolution don't need rehearsing here. However, two forward-looking points can be made in relation to such mineral investments.

Firstly, a new, more open administration is likely to seek further foreign investment in mining. As such, it is likely that existing expertise and the operation of the Eritrean National Mining Corporation (ENAMCO) will be extended, potentially with expanded areas of exploration and concessions, including along the Red Sea coast, and ultimately offshore. Secondly, in general further FDI in minerals is unlikely to be influenced by, or itself advance, regional economic integration with neighbouring states.

However, there are a couple of potential exceptions to this observation that mineral development will have little regional impact. These concern China's role in the region and Eritrea's potash industry.

a.   the expanding policy framework for Chinese investments in the Horn – mindful that China's Fujian-based Zijin Mining acquired Nevsum's Bishaa mine in late 2018, reportedly for $1.65bn. Potential links to China's 'Maritime Silk Road/Belt and Road Initiative' framework, and Beijing's growing influence in the Horn, is discussed further in Section 3 below.

b.   the second exception concerns the development of Eritrea's potash industry. Extensive potash reserves lie either side of the Ethio-Eritrean border, largely in Afar regions. Potash mine concessions were awarded and managed separately by Ethiopian and Eritrean governments. Djibouti developed its northern port of Tadjourah to handle Ethiopia's potash exports following the closure of Assab. The peace deal re-opens the possibility that potash mined in Ethiopia will be more efficiently exported via Assab. While this will further boost Eritrea's port revenues and invisible trade balance, in addition there may be long-term economies of scale in Ethio-Eritrean cooperation over potash development.

Much has been made of Danakali's Colluli potash project in Eritrea, and the possibility of a new port being created at Anfile, mid-way between Assab and Massawa, to handle potash exports. Most recently, Asmara publicised the UNDP's apparent endorsement of the developmental potential of the project, which is currently seeking $US200m investment funds.

2.2 Autarky, sanctions and the potential for integrated regional infrastructure

The rupture with Ethiopia in 1998, followed by the PFDJ's largely autarkic, inward-looking trade and developmental strategies, mean that Eritrea has relatively limited physical connections with its neighbours. Potential priorities for change include:

•   Improved road links with Ethiopia, across both northern (Tigray) and Assab links. The latter road has reportedly already been rehabilitated, PM Abiy and President Isaias making a symbolic visit to the joint border post in September 2018. However, despite reports of Ethiopian technical missions visiting Assab since, trade has not resumed. Improving road connections to Sudan, Eritrea's other principal potential trading partner, will also considerably boost trade and growth opportunities.

•   Hydroelectric power. Ethiopia currently exports electricity to Djibouti and Sudan. There is clear potential for Ethiopia to supply cheap and sustainable electricity to Eritrea, considerably reducing manufacturing costs in Eritrea, as well as boosting the profitability of ports. A key catalyst for Ethiopia to supply Djibouti hydro-electricity was not only to earn forex, but also to bring down operating costs in Djibouti's ports, which in turn benefitted Ethiopian importers. A similar logic would apply to Eritrea.

•   Transport and telecommunications. Restored air-links via Addis Ababa greatly enhance Eritrea's accessibility, both for overseas Eritreans and potential exporters. Improvements in telecoms and internet connections would boost the possibility of IT, media and e-based industries in Eritrea. This sector has developed rapidly in Ethiopia, and in Kenya in tandem with remittance and e-payments.

- Ports. A desire to diversify Ethiopia's access to ports has been a key policy refrain of Abiy Ahmed's administration. Ethiopia currently relies primarily upon Djibouti as its trade conduit. Kenya, Sudan and Somalia were all flagged as potential trade and port partners. However, the rehabilitation of Massawa and Assab are of far greater practical utility to Ethiopia. However, as stressed above, nine months after peace was signed, the actual modalities of Ethiopia's future use of Eritrea's main ports remain unclear. While the UAE army has dredged a military port facility adjacent to the airport north of Assab, the separate merchant port to the south remains largely mothballed. UAE's Dubai Ports World (DPW) interest in rehabilitating the port for Ethiopia's trade remains largely speculative. Port development, particularly in Assab, would appear a candidate for the 'Joint Investment Projects' flagged in the Jeddah accord. The UAE subsequently talked, albeit in nebulous terms, of financing Assab port infrastructure, even mooting an oil pipeline from there to highland Ethiopia. The latter seems somewhat improbable, given the colossal costs of such a project, and that the UAE company ENOC already operates an oil import terminal for Ethiopia in neighbouring Djibouti. On both port access, and the associated potential for Special Economic Zone or Free Trade Zone developments, Eritrea remains a long way behind Djibouti. Since 2013 Djibouti has secured considerable Chinese investment in a new Multi-Purpose Port and associated International Free Trade Zone. Both are connected by rail to Addis Ababa and a series of new, mostly Chinese, industrial zones in Ethiopia.

2.3 Employment opportunities, skills and migration in a 'new' Eritrean economy

Irrespective of what kind of government sits in Asmara, the core of most Eritreans' livelihoods, and thus the foundation of the economy as a whole, will remain rain-fed agriculture for the foreseeable future. As such, it remains vulnerable to the vagaries of the climate. Clearly, agricultural markets may be reformed, imports improved and potentially new export markets developed, notably in Sudan and the Arabian Peninsula. Yet the reality is that, as in Ethiopia and elsewhere on the continent, agriculture will not be able to generate adequate youth employment.

Thus, structural outward migration, even in the event of a political change and/or the scrapping of conscription, will remain a core characteristic of the Eritrean economy. Again, there is nothing unique about this. Not only is it the case in Ethiopia, but outward migration and inward flows of remittances are now one of the defining characteristics of many sub-Saharan economies. To date, there is no evidence that the authorities in Asmara have even considered formulating 'managed migration' policies, for example to negotiate temporary work permits for Eritrean nationals to the labour-importing economies of the Gulf. This may be one policy option open to a reformed administration, particularly if it retains close ties with Saudi and the Emirates.

Speculatively, one can flag three sets of questions about future migration, labour and remittance trends in Eritrea.

Firstly, might remittance flows be enhanced and used more productively? Will the 2 per cent tax be retained, or even increased, for use in reconstruction? Would this be a state-led initiative, as now, or would a decentralised, essentially private-sector remittance model be envisaged (as, for example, in Somalia)? There is now a very extensive literature and body of policy evidence on the use of remittances for development finance, and it seems likely that a reformed Eritrea could profitably reformat its remittance dependency. Either way, remittances will remain both the primary source of foreign exchange and a key channel of revenue for many Eritrean households.

This takes us back to the potential role of the private sector. Will private investments from Eritreans abroad be encouraged, or indeed incentivised via policy initiatives? If so, in which sectors? How will the profits required by those reinvesting personal and family capital in Eritrea be squared with the revised development objectives of the state?

This in turn raises a broader issue of how Eritrea's uniquely large (i.e. relative to the size of its population) and diverse diasporic presence might be used by a reformed administration in Asmara. As during the liberation struggle, it is diasporic links which may provide the most solid grounds for linguistic, family and economic ties overseas. This is true of both regional states – most obviously Ethiopia, but also the wider Horn and states of the Middle East – as well as elsewhere on the European and African continents. There are few countries without an extensive Eritrean presence, among them many professionals with extensive skills and contacts. Eritreans resident overseas have now accumulated considerable human and financial capital. This includes wide entrepreneurial experience and know-how of many sub-Saharan African economies. To what extent would any future government look to use this resource? The vast diaspora is largely a product of adversity over many decades: the war of liberation to 1991; the 1998–2018 Ethio-Eritrean War; brittle authoritarianism since 2001. Yet this adversity has produced a reality in which Eritreans and their financial capital based overseas are the country's most substantive resource; they are likely to remain so for the foreseeable future.

Concessional lending, donor and investor relations. One current constraint may change with a reformed or replacement administration. This is the government's strained relations with multilateral agencies. In the event of a successful, peaceful transition, it would seem probable that a far greater flow of grant and concessional financing would be available to Eritrea; from Western, Arabian and Asian sources.

3. Eritrea's potential regional economic relations

3.1 Economic ties with Ethiopia and Tigray

Although extensive private trade has developed between Eritrea and Tigray in the first year of peace (primarily consumer and construction goods imported into Eritrea), this has been largely unplanned and is yet to be institutionalised. The precariousness of such trade is underscored by the progressive closure of border crossings by the Eritrean authorities in early 2019. This has stymied, although not entirely stopped, such cross-border trade.

A formal bilateral trade agreement – covering tariffs and regulatory matters – is clearly required. However, given the deep friction and uncertainty around the current status of both TPLF-Asmara elite ties, and Mekelle-Addis strains within Ethiopia's federal constitution, the contents of such agreement, and both the composition of the negotiating teams and their negotiating stances, remain unclear.

Clearly, historically Tigray is inextricably tied by geography, language and politics to Eritrea. Indeed, it is all too easy to lose sight of the fact that the 1998–2018 rupture was historically unprecedented; in no preceding century were migration and trade flows broken. However, since the EPRDF took power in 1991, almost three decades of state-led growth in Mekelle has dramatically reversed the historic economic disparities between Eritrea and Tigray, with the inland province being historically poorer. In the long-term, the key issue is whether trade, economic development and investment between the two (i.e. Tigrayan- and Eritrean-owned capital) will be complementary or in competition.

3.2 Broader regional and international integration

Regionally, three factors appear of importance. Firstly, there has been an IGAD-wide commitment to enhancing regional integration in the Horn of Africa since the Ethio-Eritrean rapprochement of mid-2018. This is backed by key potential donors, from both the OECD and Arab states. However, while there is rhetorical talk of a 'regional peace dividend', the reality is that there have been no new confirmed cross-border investments, for example in ports and infrastructure, arising from the peace talks. To date, progress has been largely diplomatic; in the absence of detailed, signed practical agreements, peace pledges remain vague and rhetorical. Potential benefits could include genuine free movement of people across the region and enhanced infrastructure (potentially linked to the new African continental Free Trade Agreement).

The second issue is what role there may be for Arab- and Turkish-funded infrastructure development, as regional powers vie for patronage in the Horn. Thirdly, there are the uncertainties caused by both long-running civil war in Southern Sudan and now the change of government in Khartoum.

Internationally, two sets of issues may influence Eritrea's economic reintegration: China's rise and new Middle Eastern rivalries now being played out in the Horn.

3.3 China as an actor in the Red Sea region: what role for Eritrea?

The double symbolism of the first Ethiopian cargo ship to load and leave Massawa in September 2018 was apparent; it wasn't just that the Ethiopian Shipping Line's vessel was named 'Mekelle'. Rather, in an improbable chronological quirk, on 6 September the sale by Canada's Nevsum corporation of Eritrea's largest (copper-zinc) mine at Bishaa to Zijin, a Chinese mining company, was announced. The very next day, as peace was celebrated, ESL's bulk cargo ship 'Mekelle' was the first vessel to leave the port of Massawa. It was carrying zinc ore to China, mined from a facility which now belonged to a Chinese company.

As a major investor in Ethiopia in particular, China too has a vested interest in Ethio-Eritrea peace. Over the past five years China has become an influential international actor in the Horn of Africa and Red Sea. For Beijing, economic ties to states and ports surrounding the Red Sea and Gulf of Aden are pivotal to their global Belt and Road Initiative (BRI) policy framework. Within this, China's Maritime Silk Road Initiative seeks to promote trade and investment while consolidating its naval power on the key shipping routes linking Asia and Europe. Arguably, China's commercial presence has facilitated changes in Ethiopian, Somali and Eritrean policies, and is part of a broader configuration of US, EU and Arab policies in the region.

China's commercial presence in the Horn of Africa is underpinned by interlinked – rail, port and pipeline – infrastructure projects. The centrepiece is the 750km railway linking Ethiopia's capital Addis Ababa with the port of Djibouti. This $3.5bn project was financed 70 per cent by China Export-Import Bank and built by the China Railway Construction Corporation. In the past year the railway has cut travel time, for passengers and containers, from Ethiopia's capital to the coast to just eight hours.

Foreign companies investing in Ethiopia's new – Chinese sponsored – manufacturing zones can now import components and export finished goods to global markets via Djibouti's ports. Chinese interests are evident in Addis Ababa; including vast prestige building projects such the African Union HQ and the capital's Urban Light Railway system. Djibouti's new $590m Multi-Purpose Port at Doraleh was built, managed and part-owned by China Merchants

Group (CMG), the Hong Kong-based, parastatal conglomerate. China Merchants have owned 23.5 per cent of Djibouti's Port and Free Zone Authority since 2013.

In July 2018, Chinese officials and the leaders of Ethiopia, Rwanda, Sudan and Somalia inaugurated the Djibouti International Free Trade Zone. Eritrean representatives were, unsurprisingly, absent. Adjacent to the new port and China's naval facility, it is also managed and part-owned by China Merchants and the Corporation of Dalian, China's leading northern transhipment port. In December 2017, Chinese companies signed contracts for a Liquid Natural Gas plant and a 650km pipeline to bring gas from Chinese hydrocarbon facilities deep in Ethiopia's Ogaden province. Such extensive Chinese investment mirrors similar infrastructure development at other key port city hubs on the Maritime Silk Road, such as Gwadar in Pakistan and Duqm in Oman. However, two factors are unique to the Horn and Djibouti. Firstly, while the Gulf of Aden is a crucial transit corridor to Europe for Asian trade and Middle Eastern oil, it is also a vital telecommunications hub, at the crossroads of key African and Asian submarine fibre-optic cables. Secondly, far more significantly for geopolitics and Eritrea, since 2017 Djibouti has also been home to China's first permanent overseas naval base. Formally known as the People's Liberation Army Navy's (PLAN's) 'logistics centre', this base shares quays with the new commercial Multi-Purpose Port at Doraleh.

With the exception of the 2018 Zijin purchase of Nevsum/Bishaa, and the construction of a new Chinese embassy in Asmara, Eritrea has largely been left on the sidelines of this new development. Will this change under a reformed administration in Asmara?

3.4 Arab realignments; Yemen and new Arabian rivalries in the Horn?

As underscored in the Introduction, notwithstanding all the fanfare and diplomatic visits to Arab capitals by both Isaias and Abiy since mid-2018, a full year later neither the Eritrean public nor foreign diplomats are any clearer about the role of the Arab states. What, if anything, has been pledged economically or diplomatically by any of the parties to the peace deal? The UAE has extended cheap credit for much needed foreign exchange to Addis, and presumably Asmara too. However, for Eritrea we do not know to what extent the deals are linked to UAE use of Assab, or agreements linked to other aspects of Eritreans' involvement in the war in Yemen.

The UAE's military facilities in both Assab in Eritrea and now Berbera in Somaliland, are simultaneously linked to the deteriorating war and famine in Yemen and shifts in regional relations within the Horn. UAE and Saudi Arabia both claim to have helped broker peace between Ethiopia and Eritrea in mid-2018. What they expect in return remains unclear.

The UAE first opened their military base in Assab as relations with neighbouring Djibouti deteriorated, primarily due to a spat over the Dubai Ports World (DPW) managed and owned Doraleh Container Terminal. This dispute also partly informed DPW's investment in the port of Berbera in Somaliland. In 2018, DPW's director expressed interest in opening commercial port facilities in Assab, which, like Berbera, will primarily handle Ethiopian trade.

However, Djibouti is set to remain China's principal hub in the Horn, and the main trade gateway to Ethiopia. The rehabilitation of Berbera and Eritrea's two ports for Ethiopia's trade may attract additional Arab and Chinese investment, particularly as Chinese companies drill oil and gas deposits in Ethiopia's Somali-speaking Ogaden province and export them through a terminal and port being constructed in Djibouti, on the Gulf of Aden.

Since 2017, there have been a series of wider diplomatic and military initiatives to create new Red Sea alliances and pacts. The economic ramifications of these for Eritrea are beyond the scope of these notes. However, the most obvious potential implication is the manner in which economic and military patronage are intertwined. Just as political and financial capital from Middle Eastern states currently plays a key role in sustaining Isaias and the PFDJ, so such sources of support are likely to play a key role in the competition for power and influence in any post-Isaias administration. Potential patronage is likely to operate via well established diasporic ties, not only in Jeddah and/or Abu Dhabi, but also Qatar, Turkey and their respective influences in Sudan, Egypt, Ethiopia and Somalia.

Conclusion

In conclusion it is worth briefly restating four core points.

Firstly, when considering the constraints facing Eritrea's economy, it is useful to avoid what I'll term 'Eritrean exceptionalism'. Many of the long-term economic challenges facing Eritrea are common to all the states of the region, including Ethiopia. Such challenges include youth under-employment, precarious rain-fed agricultural production, consequent outward migration and remittance-dependency, weak export potential. More broadly, Eritrea also shares many characteristics with comparably small, poor, post-colonial African states ruptured by inter-state, and civil, wars. As such, Eritrea should seek to learn from their attempts and errors during reconstruction, while consolidating policies where the PFDJ made progress, in health for example.

Secondly, many of the challenges facing a reformed or replacement administration will be identical to those facing the current administration. This is particularly true in terms of reliance on limited FDI, foreign exchange constraints and widespread un- and under-employment, particularly for young people. Improved regional economic integration can positively assist in addressing such problems, but its impact will be necessarily limited.

Thirdly, a series of questions remain as regards any new administration's policies towards key economic policy options. These include policies towards both Eritrea's diaspora and diverse, extensive and experienced 'human capital' overseas, and what role is envisaged for private capital more generally. Both have the potential to be a key determinant of growth and economic stability in the long-run.

Fourthly, recent shifts in regional power-politics offer Eritreans an altered a set of both diplomatic and economic opportunities and constraints. These include the enhanced role of both China and Middle Eastern powers, in the Red Sea and wider region.

8. Eritrean diaspora working together

Araya Debessay

Professor of accounting, University of Delaware and member of Eritrean Global Solidarity for National Dialogue

Introduction

First and foremost, I would like to thank the organisers of the conference for taking the initiative to organise this conference on 'Building Democracy in Eritrea' at this very critical juncture of our country's history. I am grateful and feel honoured to be invited to participate at this conference.

The structure of my presentation

The organisers of the conference have rightly stated, 'The aim of the conference is to look ahead, rather than dwelling on the past'. Following this advice, I will resist the temptation of dwelling on the evil deeds of the Isaias government. Instead, the focus of my presentation will be on, '**The role of Eritreans in the diaspora in building democracy in Eritrea, and what can be done to bring them closer to be effective.**' I will emphasise three major points: (a) the removal of the current regime as a prerequisite for the transition of Eritrea to democracy, (b) the role of forces inside the country, and (c) the role of Eritreans in the diaspora. I will explain the need and the process of electing legitimate **global leadership** that will have the mandate to represent and coordinate the activities of Eritreans in the diaspora to support and to assist the forces inside the country. I will also briefly discuss my assessment and observations of strengths and weaknesses of the activities of Eritreans in the diaspora. Hoping the points I will raise will further be developed at the breakout session in detail, I will try to be brief in my presentation.

The removal of the regime as a prerequisite to build democracy in Eritrea

Eritreans have helplessly suffered under a dictatorial regime led by a brutal individual for 28 years. There is no rule of law, no institutions, no accountability. The gross violations of human rights of this regime are well known internally and internationally. Unconcerned about the incalculable damage he has caused to our country and its unsuspecting people, the dictator now appears poised to unleash another attack at the very sovereignty of our country by signing deals with foreign countries. While some of these deals threaten outright takeover of our sovereign land by foreign powers (e.g. the port of Assab), others consist of the signing of secretive agreements (e.g. the peace agreement with Ethiopia) whose consequences to the country cannot be predicted at this moment for lack of basic information.

The prospect of positive democratic change in Eritrea, in my view, is unthinkable as long as Isaias is in power. The regime has to be removed immediately if democratic changes are to take place in Eritrea. No one should be fooled by any unlikely concessions Isaias may make or may promise to make. He has made many promises in the past to prolong his stay in power. But, alas, he has flagrantly broken all of the promises he made without any concern to honour the very values that enshrine our freedom struggle. Isaias cannot be trusted. He must go.

Role of Eritreans in the diaspora

Eritreans in the diaspora can play an important role in facilitating regime change from inside the country by following a three-pronged media strategy and through lobbying, advocacy and diplomatic activities.

The three-pronged media strategy. By sending powerful and targeted messages that will (a) persuade security forces to reflect on the current political debacle with a view to refraining from executing oppressive norms and mistreating the people; (b) mobilise the civilian population to challenge the regime through peaceful demonstrations and civil disobedience; and (c) embolden the military to remove the regime with minimum collateral damage. These messages should be done skilfully by professionals using TV, radio, written material and other means of communication. To be effective, such media activities should be coordinated by legitimately elected global leaders, which I will discuss in this paper later on. What is being done so far, by various activist groups and individuals, although commendable, could be done more effectively if they were coordinated.

Preparing the groundwork for smooth transition. Due to the well-financed security apparatus of the regime, those who will remove the regime from inside will have to operate under extreme secrecy. This means they will not have the luxury to prepare detailed plans for a smooth transition in the aftermath of regime change. The global leaders, with assistance from Eritrean elders, Eritrean technocrats, intellectuals, seasoned politicians, diplomats and other advisors, can help in preparing a blueprint to ensure smooth transition. Among these tasks that require advance preparation are:

1. Maintenance of peace and order. We all know what happened in Somalia after the fall of Said Barre, or what happened in Libya after the fall of Gaddafi. Hence, to avoid a repeat of the Somalian or Libyan experiences, it will be imperative to make the necessary planning and preparation to ensure a smooth transition to democracy. The elected global leaders can help the forces inside the country by planning in advance for the maintenance of peace and order in the aftermath of regime change.

2. Planning for smooth transition. The global leaders will be expected to assist the forces inside the country in the following important tasks, among others, in order to ensure a smooth transition in the aftermath of regime change:

   a. Planning for an all-inclusive National Conference within the shortest possible time frame.

   b. Establishing procedures for the election of a Constituent Assembly.

   c. Mobilising knowledgeable and experienced technocrats who can assist the caretaker transitional government in jumpstarting the various sectors of the economy, in the management of the banking sector and the various government entities that provide vital services such as addressing public health, food security of the population, etc.

4. Advocacy, lobbying and diplomacy. The third important activity that can be done by the global leaders representing Eritreans in the diaspora is in the lobbying, advocacy and diplomatic arena. Although Eritreans in the diaspora have shown their commitment to helping their people by conducting demonstrations, writing petitions, appearing in congressional hearings, at UN meetings in Geneva and in New York, writing letters to the Prime Minister of Ethiopia Abiy Ahmed, etc., the outcome has not been very effective. These measures were taken by dedicated activists or groups, which are commendable; however, they could have had a greater chance of being heard more seriously if they were coordinated and conducted by a leadership that has the legitimacy and the mandate to speak for and represent Eritreans in the diaspora.

An important advocacy, lobbying and diplomatic work that can be done by the global leaders or an appointed group of high-calibre experienced Eritreans is to convince the international community in general and the UN, AU, EU, the Arab League and IGAD, in particular, to support the Eritrean people's demand for social and political change. These organisations and the international community as a whole must understand that Isaias is not a constitutionally and democratically elected leader. He has ruled the country with an iron fist for over 28 years, without any constitutional mandate. He has committed serious human rights violations against his people that are properly documented by the United Nations Human Rights Enquiry Commission that amount to crimes against humanity. The world should understand that the Eritrean people have no other option but to remove this ruthless dictator by any means possible. He has taken power illegally, hence, he is a usurper, and as such he has no moral or legal ground to defend his dictatorship. We have to convince the international community Isaias is an illegitimate 'leader' and a violator of all human rights and related principles that are honoured by the family of nations.

Once elected, the global leaders, with the mandate given to them, should negotiate with the foreign powers to get much needed assistance to jumpstart the ruined economy of the country.

The elected global leaders will be expected to have serious discussions with the leaders of the Ethiopian government. They should stress that democratic Eritrea after Isaias will certainly want to live in peace and harmony with Ethiopia, in a context of two neighbourly sovereign countries operating for peace and development of their respective economies and societies. The agreements that will be made between these two countries will have to be based on these principles. Any agreement made with Isaias cannot be endorsed by the democratic government of Eritrea, if it contradicts the above stated principles.

Soft landing option

The soft landing option was an idea suggested by Abderahman Said (Bohashem) in an article titled 'How to achieve soft landing' posted at Awate.com on 15 May 2007. Bohashem argued on the merits of offering Isaias a 'soft landing', citing Nelson Mandela who was praised for 'achieving justice without seeking vengeance'.

In the Eritrean context, the soft landing option means approaching Isaias directly or indirectly through intermediaries and offering him the option to relinquish power voluntarily with the assurance of his safety, immunity from prosecution and a good retirement package. This offer is best handled by the elected global leaders who have the legitimacy and the mandate to speak on behalf of Eritreans in the diaspora and the voiceless inside the country. I understand that, to many Eritreans, the idea of offering Isaias a soft landing is a bitter pill to swallow. But we should recognise that it is highly unlikely that Isaias will seriously consider any soft landing option to relinquish power voluntarily. However, there is a lot to gain but little to lose from such a step of attempting to resolve a national crisis through a peaceful approach. The expected rejection of an olive branch will further expose Isaias in the eyes of the international community and all peace-loving people, including from his hardcore supporters. By contrast, the very fact that the Eritrean people are willing to consider a peaceful way of ending their country's political problems will gain the Eritrean people considerable goodwill and will justify any other means to remove the regime.

An assessment of the strengths of Eritreans in the diaspora

When one considers the number of Eritreans who participate in demonstrations against the regime, in Geneva, Israel, Addis Ababa, New York City, Washington DC and other places, some traveling across a continent despite their meagre financial resources; and when one observes the large number of Eritreans who spend hours in Pal Talk rooms on a daily basis, discussing the conditions in the country, one is left with the unmistakable impression that Eritreans in the diaspora are indeed deeply troubled with what is going on in their country. In short, there is overwhelming evidence that indicates the intensity of the support of Eritreans in the diaspora to bring changes in their country, particularly after the recent outrageous actions of Isaias that are threatening the very sovereignty of our country. Young professionals are coming up to the fold with impactful initiatives, such as One Nation, Renaissance, Bright Future, etc., using social media and modern technology. The recent chain of video messages, stating 'enough is enough', that is circulating around the world like wildfire is sufficient evidence about the desire of Eritreans in the diaspora to bring positive changes in their country. In addition, there are also many civic organisations, political parties and individual initiatives that are exposing the ruthlessness and viciousness of Isaias's regime. All these activities are commendable and these are manifestations of the interest of Eritreans in the diaspora in ending the suffering of their people. In addition, Eritreans in the diaspora have done a lot to support their extended family members through their remittances that are sustaining the lives of those who do not have any means of survival, while unfortunately giving the regime an essential lifeline for its existence.

An assessment of the major weaknesses of Eritreans in the diaspora

Despite the strong evidence of the interest of justice-seeking Eritreans in their country's affairs, so far, they have not been effective to bring about any positive changes in their country. This is primarily because they are operating in a fragmented fashion and their activities and actions are not properly coordinated. There are many political opposition groups, too many for a small country, who claim to have the same objectives and aspirations but, unfortunately, they have not been able to work together. Likewise, we have a multitude of civic organisations that are operating separately. The lack of coordination among these various groups has rendered them ineffective in playing a critical role in bringing about fundamental changes in the country.

What needs to be done to bring the Eritrean diaspora closer together?

There is an urgent need of the various activist constituent groups to agree on the need of electing global leaders to coordinate their activities.

The process of forming legitimate global leaders

For the global leaders to be truly legitimate leaders with the mandate to represent diaspora Eritreans, it is critically important that all Eritreans in every part of the globe, particularly the members of the various activist groups listed below, participate in the election process. What has rendered diaspora Eritreans ineffective, so far, has been their fragmentation. Ideally, the process of electing legitimate global leaders should start at the grassroots level, where members of all the below listed constituent groups and political parties have an opportunity to participate in the election process as members of their respective communities regardless of their party or group affiliation. I am not advocating the disbanding of these constituent groups, what I am urging is the need of their participation in the election process in their respective geographical areas. This will require an intensive campaign to mobilise and reach out to **ALL** Eritreans in every locality irrespective of their gender, religion, ethnicity, region and political affiliation.

Once Eritreans in every corner of the world elect their local leaders, the next step for these elected leaders is to meet and elect their country-wide representatives. This process should take place in every country and every continent.

The final step is to have a global conference of Eritrean representatives from every corner of the world – Africa, Asia, Australia, Europe, Middle East, North America, South America and other places – to elect the Eritrean global leaders. Below is a list of activist groups who have been operating independently.

1.   Eritrean opposition political parties.

2.   Eritrean women.

3.   Eritrean lawyers.

4.   Eritrean youth: One Nation, Renaissance, Bright Future, etc.

5.   Eritrean intellectuals – Eritrean Global Solidarity for National Dialogue (EGSND).

6.   Eritrean artists and musicians.

7.   Eritrean minority ethnic groups, and those that have formed regional or religious associations.

8.   Members of Eritrean civic organisations, such as Human rights activists, members of Eritrean community centres, and other civic associations.

9.   Eritrean website masters, radio and TV programme managers and Pal Talk administrators.

10.   Eritrean activists that do not belong to any of the above groups.

The role of diaspora Eritreans in post-Isaias Eritrea

It should be clear from the outset that Eritreans in the diaspora are not meant to become the leaders of the country by virtue of their position of strength in terms of their level of education, experience and capital resources. It is the Eritrean people who should choose their leaders. Likewise, it should also be clear that the individuals who are now leaders of the opposition groups, particularly the senior citizens, are not meant, ipso facto, to be placed in a position of leadership. We need to make these points a priority in order to facilitate the emergence of sustainable democracy and development. Nowadays, many African countries appear to have understood that senior people should hand over power to the next generation, and the average age of African leaders is steadily coming down. Isaias was one of the youngest African leaders in the early 1990s, but he is now one of the oldest. Our young and middle-aged citizens should be given the opportunity to lead the country. Our senior citizenry can positively play an advisory and watchdog role as related to the progress in implementing democratic norms, respect of human rights and protection and preservation of the environment. The leaders of Eritreans in the diaspora are better positioned to perform those functions. The fact that the leaders are outside can help them to be objectively critical of any wrongdoing by the newly elected leaders without fearing vengeful actions by the government authorities. Accordingly, they can continue to be effective advocates of democratic and human rights values on behalf of the Eritrean people, and keep the democratisation process moving forward.

Of course, Eritreans in the diaspora will be expected to contribute to the economic development of the country through their investments in the various industrial sectors.

Summary and conclusion

To summarise and conclude, the time is ripe to remove the dictatorial regime before our hard-won sovereignty is compromised. The regime has to go by any means possible. And it is the forces of change inside the country that are in a position to remove the regime. But Eritreans in the diaspora can also play an important role in the process of regime change and in helping the forces inside the country by preparing a blueprint to ensure that there is a smooth transition to democracy in the aftermath of regime change. This requires all justice-seeking Eritreans in the diaspora to work together by forming a legitimate global leadership that is given the mandate to represent them and that will coordinate their activities. For the legitimacy of the global leaders it is important that they are elected through the participation of all justice-seeking Eritreans in every part of the world.

Asia Abdulkadir

Gender consultant, UN Development Programme and chair of the Network of Eritrean Women

Dr Asia Abdulkadir (Credit: Martin Plaut)

How can the capacity of civic organisations be improved to address the needs of Eritrean people from a gender perspective?

In recent years, we have noticed growing formations of civic organisations representing women, youth and minority groups in the diaspora. Eritrean women's rights initiatives are not only working to expose government's cruelty towards women, but they also engage and sensitise the opposition groups in gender equality issues.

Most of the civic organisations work in difficult and challenging circumstances with limited resources and constantly changing, complex and dynamic situations. Women human rights defenders have been facing threats of violence. Sometimes they are targeted for being activists, and sometimes just for being women.

From women's perspective, apart from the geographical distance and lack of funding, one of the main challenges in the context of Eritrean civic organisations is the concept of 'Hade Libi Hade hizbi' – 'One heart one people'. Many in the male dominated opposition movement believe that the formation of interest-based groups such as women and youth initiatives is weakening the struggle for change and freedom in Eritrea. The perception is that the country is at risk therefore we should fight together instead of being represented in diverse groups. This approach is problematic as the experiences and grievances of women with the regime in Eritrea are different, therefore women need a protected space to work on matters that affect their lives.

Moreover, opposition groups lack capacity to engage women meaningfully. Women are often invited by opposition groups to participate in conferences and projects without involving them in the agenda setting and decision-making processes. In some instances, when women demanded gender to be included in the agenda of the conference, they were asked to discuss gender issues during lunch break.

The above-presented experiences have caused frustration among women activists. That means understanding the opportunities and constraints faced by women's initiatives in the struggle for gender equality is increasingly important. The creation of interest-based groups such as the Network of Eritrean Women (NEW) and youth movements, etc., should be given high priority. Without institutional and cultural shifts with dedicated and robust investment in gender mainstreaming and gender equality, little could change.

Way forward and recommendations

Meaningful participation requires that women are entitled to participate in the decisions that directly affect them, including in the design, implementation and monitoring of health interventions. In practice, meaningful participation may take on a number of different forms, including:

- representation/quotas;
- attendance in meetings (physical presence);
- influencing discussions;
- agenda setting;
- decision-making.

We need to increase knowledge of representation of women and youth in the opposition movement. Moving beyond the numbers or percentages is more critical. We need to focus on the qualitative component of women's participation.

We need to provide tools on gender equality for political parties and the leaders of civic organisations.

Strengths

Ownership, not donor driven.

Weaknesses

Lack of capacity to run a professional organisation, lack of coordinating body and lack of funds to enhance the capacity of civil society organisations.

9. The empowerment of women and youth

Abeba T. Baatai

Eritrean fighter and human rights activist

Abeba T. Baatai (Credit: Martin Plaut)

Youth and women's empowerment

Across the board, women as a demographic group make up half of the human population, but they are economically, politically and socially marginalised, especially in poor and conflict-ridden societies – Eritrean women are not different. Eritrean culture emphasises the domesticity of women, confining their role to tending to their husband, children and home.

Although they had to fight an uphill battle for recognition and equality, women fighters, a third of the army, served alongside their counterparts, proving themselves through heroic action in combat. Besides distinguishing themselves by their bravery in combat, Eritrean women played a critical role in providing logistic support and military intelligence, and caring for wounded fighters behind enemy lines. Further, they served vital roles in supporting various fields crucial for the success of the liberation struggle, including mass communication (Dimtsi Hafash), education, administration, agriculture, medical and construction.

The Eritrean liberation movement recognised the fundamental importance and potential role of women to win the liberation struggle. Even so, women were relegated to serving in lower ranks in the military infrastructure. Further, gender equality and women's empowerment were not an integral part of the vision for a progressive, democratic and developed Eritrean society after independence, as evidenced by the lack of support structures such as financial welfare or professional training to facilitate the transition and reintegration of veteran women into society and ensure their self-sufficiency. As for the rest of women in Eritrean society – they were, once again, relegated to domestic roles.

Gender-based violence was rampant during the liberation struggle, perpetuated both by the ruling Dergue regime and the EPLF commanders. Today, women in the national service (agelgelot) continue to experience physical or sexual abuse at the hands of those who are supposed to provide leadership. This can have lifelong repercussions for women by undermining their physical and mental health and eroding their dignity and self-worth. Eritrean women have been forced to have unwanted pregnancies, sexually transmitted diseases and other reproductive health issues. Those that flee the country to avoid national service have faced a worse fate at the hands of traffickers and smugglers.

There is currently no democratic governance in Eritrea. In its 21 June 2017 resolution, the United Nations High Commission for Human Rights reported serious concerns about human rights in Eritrea and recommended an investigation into violations that may be considered crimes against humanity. Women's rights are human rights and there cannot be women's empowerment where every citizen is disempowered.

For women to have gender equality and empowerment the following points are important:

1. Establish a democratic government where gender equality and women's empowerment are embedded in the constitution. We should never forget the bitter experience we had due to our failure to build institutions and ratify and implement relevant legislation. A democratic Eritrea should promote women's right to live free from gender-based violence and abuse.

2. The 28 years of dictatorship created mistrust and discord among citizens, using mainly religion and ethnicity to divide people. So, every Eritrean should take responsibility and work for peace building, starting by self-transformation. The peace building process must start now, and the inclusion of women should be mandatory.

3. Creating a strong organisation that stands for women's rights and promotes full participation of women in socioeconomic activities must be a national priority.

4. Boys were given priority to go to school; now we must create an environment where girls are encouraged to go to school and work to remove all barriers to school attendance.

5. We should encourage women in the diaspora who are highly educated and working in different professions to go back to their homeland to serve their people – with adequate remuneration – and concentrate on making it conducive for women to attain higher education and have full participation in government and businesses.

6. As noted above, Eritrean people have suffered for many years, but women have suffered exponentially due to gender-based violence. Telling their stories openly and writing books about it can be a process for healing; and for society to ensure that such atrocities never happen again.

Meron Semedar

International speaker and advocate with first-hand experience of the infamous indefinite national service and human rights violations

Eritrean youth: a force for change and a bright future

[This contribution was read at the conference in its entirety by Helen Kidane]

Abstract

Throughout history, it was proven that the youth are the backbone of any nation. Eritrean youth have also been instrumental since its inception in protecting and building their country against all odds. The Eritrean youth of today, although faced with many challenges, continue to fight for freedom and democracy from different corners of the world. In this paper, I will be discussing the historical and current involvement of Eritrean youth in relation to their country. Strong focus will be given to the role of millennial Eritreans in the current struggle for change and youth empowerment. This paper was produced for a conference organised by Eritrea Focus (Exposing human rights abuses in Eritrea) and the Institute of Commonwealth Studies at the School of Advanced Study, University of London.

Defining the term 'youth'

The United Nations defines 'youth' as being an indication of a person 'between the age where he/she may leave compulsory education, and the age at which he/she finds his/her first employment' (UN Charter). According to the UN, the youth group are 'persons between the age of 15 to 24 years'. Whereas the African Union Charter defines the age group of youth being an individual between the ages of 15 and 35 (African Union Youth Charter). Referring to the different age group definitions in the UN and the AU charters, we first need to ask, which age group can truly represent youth in the Eritrean demography? The UN age group does apply to the Eritreans who are born in diaspora, but not those inside the country. Understanding to the historical situation of Eritrea, for the purpose of this paper and especially in the definition of the current Eritrean youth (millennial, born and raised in Eritrea), we will use the African Charter age category.

Short history of Eritrean youth

Pre-colonial era, Eritrean youth, besides their daily activity for sustenance, played a role of defending their regions governed by traditional leaders. The era of Italian colonisation brought the name and boundaries of Eritrea, in which many youths – some voluntarily to fulfil their pride and some forced – joined the Italian army to fight the wars of the coloniser in places such as Somalia, Ethiopia and Libya. This time was also known for the era of apartheid in Eritrea in which Eritreans were considered as second-class citizens and were not allowed to use services that a white person uses.

The end of World War Two brought a time of political awareness and exercise in Eritrea. During the British administration, four vibrant political parties were created by the youth of the day. Although the 1940s and 1950s youth generation were politically active, their lack of unity for independence opened the opportunity for emperor Haile Selassie to dissolve Eritrea's Parliament and annexe the country with Ethiopia. Although this generation had its faults, they also laid the ground for the start of armed struggle in the early 1960s.

The rise of tens of thousands of Eritrean youth from the early 1960s to 1980s brought a great deal of victory in which a huge sacrifice was also made. This era refers to the youth of the Eritrean Liberation Front (ELF) and Eritrean People's Liberation Front (EPLF). Mainly due to the courageous sacrifice and determination of this youth generation, today we have a sovereign and independent country that we belong to. However, this generation also came with their own faults and the victory that they brought was short lived. The urge to go to war with almost every neighbouring country, the miscalculation and unnecessary border war with Ethiopia, the lack of implementing the 1997 ratified Constitution, the arrest of G15, closing of Asmara university and private medias, arresting dozens of innocent journalists. The list is endless. This period officially marked the era of dictatorship in Eritrea.

In post-independence Eritrea, especially in the early years of the 1990s, there were many youths in the cities with too much time on their hands. In the big cities, there were continuous fights between the different areas of the cities led by the youth. It was also a time of active sport competition in which the stadiums during soccer matches and the city streets during cycling competitions on Sundays were full of too many young people. The declaration of the proclamation of national service in which every adult person was required to perform 18 months' national service were initially widely accepted by the society. As such, the proclamation was very successful in the early first to fourth rounds. This proclamation also gave the youth of the 1990s a chance to truly serve their country happily. My personal witness is that I saw my neighbour asking his mother to voluntarily register and send him off to Sawa military training on the day of the second round departure. This generation, which we refer to as 'Warsay', serving from first to 13th round, was tested by fire in a war in which they never had a say, but they had to fight and defend their country. Today many of the youth who defended Eritrea's boarder against Ethiopia after spending years in the national service have fled the country and are in different corners of the world to lead their lives peacefully. Many are also still serving in the national service with little pay in the hopes of being discharged. The longest serving are the fifth round, which has been in the army for more than 21 years consecutively.

The other generation of the 1990s youth can be described as the ones who joined the only Asmara university in the country. Although very few in comparison with the total population, it is only this generation in the history of Eritrea that benefited from the strong educational system that existed in the country. Many members of this generation were also sent to second and first world countries for better education, such as South Africa. However, for those in South Africa, due to a heated debate that they had with the president, their scholarship and ultimately their education was disrupted by the regime in Asmara and the Eritrean embassy in South Africa. It is also in the time of this generation that private media flourished in Eritrea, that played a leading role in raising many important questions about the country's affairs. These newspapers, although short lived, played a leading role in the social and political empowerment of the people. Today, it can be safely concluded an estimated 80 to 90 per cent of those who studied or graduated from Asmara University have fled the country and live in Europe, North America, Australia and South Africa and many other parts of the world. However, the worrying part is that only very few of these students/graduates of Asmara University have been and are actively involved in the struggle for freedom or in leading and empowering Eritrean communities in the diaspora.

What followed was the current generation of millennial (those born in the 1980s and 1990s to the early 2000s) which served from the 14th to the current 32nd round of national service in Eritrea. It is during the time of this generation that Eritrea's route to dictatorship became very clear, in 2001. The closure of Asmara University, in 2003, followed by the change in the education system in which every grade 11 student at the end of the their high school year was forced to do grade 12 and military training at the Sawa military training camp, starting with the 16th round of national service. I for one fit in this generation having joined the 18th round of national service in 2004. The common discussion among this generation while still in high school is that, 'all the hard work is for Sawa'. Noting from their previous generation's example, most of this generation know way before they finish grade 11 that achieving their dream through education in Eritrea is not going to be a reality. Hence, many embark on fleeing the country before they even finish high school. Some use Sawa as a route to freedom due to its proximity to the border with Sudan. Many young girls end up getting married due to pressure from parents to avoid going to Sawa. It is this generation who have been fleeing the country in floods for the last decade and a half. On route to safety, this generation faced a shoot to kill policy at the Eritrean border, dealing with smugglers, being held hostage at the hands of human and organ traffickers, crossing the Sahara Desert, the Mediterranean Sea and languishing in a desolate refugee camp. The agony of this generation continues as they reach what they thought would be their final destination. Having to integrate in a society and culture that is nothing like home. Having to learn a new language, a new way of life and for many to prove to their host country that they fear persecution should they return to Eritrea. This youth generation today carry the trauma inherited from their own government in Eritrea and the harrowing experience faced in their journey to safety.

Collecting the youth from all corners of Eritrea in Sawa does expose them to learning team work and developing tolerance for the multilingual, multi-ethnic and religious groups that exist. However, the indefinite national service has destroyed the fabric of Eritrean society, making children grow up without a father figure and spouses always separated. Many also were denied the pursuit of life progress such as getting a job, being independent, getting married or having children.

Many Eritrean youth have been wasting their precious time in a senseless border patrol due to the repressive regime policies for the last two decades. After learning the national service will not allow them to better their life, they end up escaping the country to seek a better life elsewhere. For those who give the education system a try hoping things will change in the process, once they notice it has not changed, they flee the country after completing their first degree. My best friend Girmay, after seven years of studying for medical school and serving more than two years of national service, could not pay his own rent and decided to flee the country. Girmay was also not allowed to work outside the government hospital in his spare time. Such is the story of millennial Eritreans. Young people like Girmay know that they cannot practice their profession in the diaspora due to the nature of their field, but they still choose to flee for their freedom.

Today it is safe to declare that Eritrea lost most of its productive youth firstly fighting in the senseless border war with Ethiopia, then trying to flee the country and reach a safe country. The United Nations refugee agency, UNHCR, reported '474,296 Eritreans globally to be refugees and asylum seekers at the end of 2015, about 12 percent of Eritrea's official 3.6 million population estimate' (HRW, 2016). The Eritrean Catholic bishops in their pastoral letter titled 'Where is your brother?' openly summarised what happened to the youth population in Eritrea in 2014 by clearly stating that Eritrea has become a nation of elderly women and children with no one to care for them.

The other Eritrean youth of the current generation are those who were born in diasporas as a result of their families fleeing the war for independence in the 1980s. Unlike the Eritrea-born youth, this group is exposed to vast information, opportunities and has plenty of life choices to make. However, the issue of identity for this group is clear. Hence, they are an easy target for PFDJ to be recruited as members and to serve for the government propaganda. Very few but also some vibrant members of this group stand out as a voice for freedom and justice for their brothers and sisters in Eritrea.

Youth in leadership

The National Union of Eritrean Youth and Students (NUEYS), although it prides itself on being democratic, non-profit and nongovernmental, in reality is completely controlled and operated by the People's Front for Democracy and Justice (PFDJ) – the only political administration in Eritrea. A sister to this organisation is the YPFDJ (Y for young), which operates out of the diasporas and often holds political seminars, entertainment and group visits to their homeland.

In general, it is safe to conclude no Eritrean youth have held any middle or higher political leadership role in the current administration. For the last 27 years the voice of the youth has been silenced by the administration in power. As a result, every now and then there have been small but non-impactful protests inside the country such as the Asmara University protesters in the early 2000s who were sent to Wia and Gahtelay as a punishment, and the 18th round Sawa military training camp protesters in 2004 who were punished by being forced to climb mountains in Sawa.

Eritreans demanding freedom and justice have set up many organisations over the years to combat dictatorship in Eritrea from the diaspora. Among them the Eritrean Movement for Democracy and Human Rights (EMDHR) based in South Africa, Eritrean Youth for Change (EYC) based in Oakland, Eritrean Youth Solidarity for National Salvation (EYSNS or Simret) based in Ethiopia, Eritrean Women for Change based mostly in Europe and North America, Eritrean Youth Solidarity for Change (EYSC) global. Another youth led organisation is Arbi Harinet, with members both inside Eritrea (invisible to the regime in Asmara) and outside the country. A youth wing of the Eritrean National Council for Democratic Change (ENCDC) also convened in Hawassa in 2012 (Mohammad and Tronvoll, 2015). A common phenomenon with all these organisations is that they start out very ambitious and most of them with democratic leadership. However, the leadership role soon fractures and both leaders and members of the organisations split over differences. New groups continue to be formed by different groups. Their sustainability is yet to be tested. The historic lesson of these organisations raises some questions, such as:

1.   What was the impact of these organisations in comparison to their objective?
2.   What is the reason for their lack of sustainability?

In the average Eritrean household, young people do not have much of a say. Decisions for young people are made usually by parents or guardians. This is coupled with the socio-cultural dynamics of the society playing a leading role as a hurdle for younger people to shine as leaders of their community. The different historical context between the youth who fled Eritrea since 2001 and those who fled the country in the 1980s also plays an active role.

Recommendation on youth policy and framework

The following policies are needed to ensure that Eritrean youth are an integral part of the society and that their issues and needs are addressed.

So far, the framework towards youth in Eritrea has been from the point of PFDJ leaders which often pride themselves by stating, 'you will learn what we want you to learn, because we know what is good for this country'. In this process they denied the youth of fulfilling their dreams and imagination. Yes, PFDJ did create opportunity for eradicating illiteracy and a college system education. However, such an educational system was created to teach students 'what to think' instead of 'how to think'. In post-dictatorship Eritrea, the education system needs to be revamped with a new image for a bright future.

The youth who made a perilous journey to the diasporas need to empower themselves by learning the local languages and going to universities. This would make them useful and empower them to lead Eritrea tomorrow. Also, a personal responsibility should be taken by the older generation of scholars in the diasporas to guide and encourage the newcomers to go to school and provide resources. Within the Eritrean community in the diasporas, we also need to recognise role models who could set an example for the new arrivals. This could be done by annually recognising and prizing those who have achieved great progress despite their circumstances. Books and entertainment (such as sport and musical materials) should be collected from the diasporas and distributed to the Eritrean refugees in different refugee camps.

The framework of governance in Eritrea should allow for and encourage youth participation in public office. This way the youth themselves can best represent and protect their rights. In the future democratic Eritrea, a body of youth parliament must be created and convene at least twice annually to represent the voice of the youth at the highest level.

The indefinite national service which often is termed as 'modern slavery' has been one of the main driving forces for the youth to flee Eritrea. Should the national service continue, it needs to be limited to the stated 18 months. The youth who have been serving for more than this period also needs to be compensated in some form to make up for the extra years spent.

Due to the socio-cultural belief and lack of awareness, the youth of today continues to live with excessive trauma and PTSD. In the United States, we have started recognising the need to address this and have made some progress by inviting Eritrean scholars in the field to come and educate the communities. Similar work could be done in other countries. Because the best assets we have are scholars within our community, we need to fund them and encourage them to work with the traumatised generation. Also, every community needs to collaborate with NGOs in their respective cities who specialise in the field. In every household we need to talk about trauma, normalise the issue as any other sickness and break the old belief of taboo. Beyond the personal, we need to recognise the 'collective trauma' as a society we Eritrean have suffered and continue to suffer from. Religious places which have a big influence in the diaspora need to create a safe space for people of trauma and provide support and comfort.

The youth of today need to understand that at the root of their problem is the lack of freedom and democracy in Eritrea. Only their cooperation and brotherhood could end the situation. Hence, they need to work with one another, respecting their personal rights. Developing tolerance, a team work ethic, reading books, understanding Eritrean history and recognising that we are all part of the problem and facing the consequence together would most likely produce a way forward for cooperation and networking among youth.

During the last few years, Eritrean refugees in Ethiopian refugee camps have played a pivotal role in addressing the need for peace and worked on many collaborative and celebratory events to ease the tension with their host community. Their work should be encouraged and continued until the day they are repatriated. Donations and funding should be made by the diaspora Eritreans to encourage such activity.

The youth, noting that the future belongs to them, need to be the catalyst of positive change in Eritrea. First to end the era of dictatorship through a non-violent means such as civil disobedience and peaceful protest, as was the case in Sudan, Tunisia and Egypt. They also need to show restraint in times of peaceful transition and picture the bright future ahead. Those in diasporas need to exercise their full right to a peaceful protest to address the need for change in Eritrea and have a civilised discussion with their counterparts such as the YPFDJ. However, more than anything, they need to use the opportunities available in diasporas to educate themselves. This way, they will not only empower themselves, but will also become leaders of their households and communities and steer the discussion to bring a positive peace.

In a highly religious society like Eritrea, religious leaders should play an active role in empowering and guiding our youth from falling for the wrong motives.

The media in diaspora such as Assena and Erena should provide a programme for the youth to educate, empower and for their voice to be heard.

Artist youth in part should play an active role in being the voice of their generation through the medium of music, drama, comedy, etc.

Conclusion

In conclusion, looking at Eritrean youth history through generation after generation, it becomes clear that every generation struggles to correct the mistakes of the previous generation. The youth of today are paying a heavy price and continue to do so as a result of mistakes made by their predecessors.

Today's youth work is to secure freedom and democracy in Eritrea and the future generations' work is to sustain it. Understanding that freedom is not given but earned and the future belongs to them, the youth needs to act now and make history by snatching the torch of freedom from the hands of those denying them. Hence, they need to lead this struggle from the front.

Every generation of the Eritrean society should assist in empowering and guiding the youth of today. The youth are our hope and we need to invest in them.

Citations

Definition of Youth, UN https://www.un.org/esa/socdev/documents/youth/fact-sheets/youth-definition.pdf

The African Youth Charter, CARMMA http://www.carmma.org/resource/african-youth-charter

Eritrea: Events of 2016, HRW (2016) https://www.hrw.org/world-report/2017/country-chapters/eritrea

Yebio, G. *A few words on the 'Pastoral Letter' by the Catholic Bishops of Eritrea*, Asmarino (2014) http://www.asmarino.com/articles/2103-a-few-words-on-the-qpastoral-letterq-by-the-catholic-bishops-of-eritrea

Mohammad, A.S. and Tronvoll, K. *Eritrean opposition parties and civic organisations*, NOREF (2015) *Norwegian Peacebuilding Resource Centre Expert Analysis.*

10. The media, freedom of expression and the right to information

Abraham Zere

Journalist and executive director, PEN Eritrea

'At least now we can speak and maybe be heard': the role of social media in challenging Eritrea's political repression

Abstract

Eritrea's repressive media-sphere has been widely documented, placing the country 10 years in a row at the bottom of the World Press Freedom Index, in the yearly survey of Reporters Without Borders. Although there are many reports that deal with how the Eritrean regime has silenced traditional media, little has been written about how social media has been utilised to break the silence on Eritrea. By taking the popular Arab Spring as a point of comparison, Eritrea offers a unique ground to assess how social media can still be crucial in an extremely closed system with very little access where the state habitually resorts to lethal force to squash any dissidence. I have conducted the research using three methods of qualitative research and my findings reveal that despite all the challenges Eritrean social media sites have helped in conquering fear, sharing information, mobilising resources and delegitimising the pariah state. I argue social media have played major role in exposing the vulnerability of the seemingly 'untouchable' regime and laid the ground for change. I conclude that the furthest role social media can play is to create platform, but it needs further impetus to secure lasting change.

Introduction

From the first independent newspaper, *Setit*, that was launched in August 1997, until the final ban of all private media on 18 September 2001, Eritreans witnessed a vibrant but short-lived newspaper era. At one point, 18 private newspapers operated in the country (Berhane, 2016).

Following the ban of seven independent newspapers and the subsequent arrests of their editors, Eritrean journalism entered a long, dark period. According to the official records of the Committee to Protect Journalists (2018), 16 independent journalists have been held, without ever having been brought into an independent court, since September 2001. They have had no contact with their families, and their whereabouts remain unknown. The September 2001 crackdown opened a dark phase in the political and cultural scene of the country. The national assembly was suspended and the state media filled the media vacuum by disseminating robust propaganda. Under President Isaias Afwerki, who has ruled the country since its independence in 1993, and the People's Front for Democracy and Justice (PFDJ) party, civil society organisations and NGOs are banned, international media correspondents are not allowed access, and political parties are barred (Tronvoll, 2009; Gagliardone and Stremlau, 2011).

Since the ban of private media, Eritrea has excavated new depths in the context of Africa. Gagliardone and Stremlau describe the atmosphere thus: 'It is the only country on the continent with no private media outlets, and the state-owned media are vehicles for aggressive propaganda celebrating the country's fighters and the government's political project, which is based on self-sufficiency and resistance to external influences' (2011, p.11).

On top of the media and private newspaper ban, Eritrea's Ministry of Information enacted and enforced pervasive censorship. According to the Ministry of Information's directives, all works to be distributed, printed and recorded in the country must get prior approval from the ministry. The lack of clear directives, combined with long waiting periods – where one film might take about a year trudging through the censorship process – has crippled Eritrean art production. Most talented writers, journalists and artists were forced to either hibernate or flee the country (Zere, 2017).

Eritrea has held a spot among the worst in rankings that document press freedom. In its 2015 survey, Committee to Protect Journalists (CPJ) named Eritrea the most censored country on earth, followed by North Korea (2015). Similarly, the country came in last, 180 among 180, in the annual Press Freedom Index compiled by Reporters Without Borders. After Eritrea secured the last place for 10 consecutive years, only in 2017 and 2018 did it see its place taken over by North Korea (Reporters Without Borders, 2017; Reporters Without Borders, 2018). Eritreans inside the country have been further disconnected due to slow internet connection, with an estimated 1.3 per cent penetration rate (Internet World Stats, 2019).

For years, through state-controlled media, the Eritrean government has succeeded in shaping its narratives. That helped the regime to effectively isolate its citizens from the international community. The lack of independent media further kept Eritreans from communicating horizontally, which in turn helped the regime continue its reign unimpeded.

So far there has not been any research on how social media is challenging the state repression in Eritrea. This is attributed to the lack of access to information and the consequent unavailability of data, due to the nature of their government. As an extension of their media control mechanisms, internet penetration is very low. Yet, I argue, the lack of better internet penetration does not necessarily mean social media platforms have been ineffective. Horizontal channels of communication, combined with citizens' growing appetite to access any decentralised information – often as an expression of bold defiance against state imposition – make social media's outreach and influence far greater than previously assumed.

Social media has abolished the geographical gap, helping to embrace the influential diaspora communities in the struggle for change. The role of the diaspora community is vital both in challenging the status quo and amplifying the demand for change.

Methodology

The research has combined multiple approaches of qualitative research. Ten prominent exiled Eritrean social media activists have been interviewed. The first set of interviews was conducted right after the Geneva demonstration of 2016. As the demonstration drew arguably the largest turn out in justice-seeking camp and owing to the fact that it was mainly coordinated through the social media platforms, it holds special importance. Coordinators of the demonstration and other social media activists who have been covering it using available social media platforms, mainly Live Facebook, have been interviewed. The second set of interviews was conducted with six leading social media activists in April 2019. Subjects were selected based on their active involvement on social media, where many also combine other platforms such as traditional media, or members of some civic organisations.

In addition to interviews, my long-term participatory observation of Eritrean social media helped me understand the dynamic better. In order to systematically categorise it, I applied Norman Fairclough's (1992) Critical Discourse Analysis (CDA) to study the most popular social media sites: Facebook, Twitter and YouTube. I chose to apply Fairclough's CDA as it is concerned with power relationships and the use of language in power dynamics. Social media being a facilitator of nonviolent struggle that heavily depends on the use of language and power, this theory helped me understand how Eritrean social media activists are employing language to challenge power.

My research focuses on the political aspect of social media in the selected three platforms.

Literature review

With the advent of social media, essential information that was once solely produced, sifted and disseminated through corporate or state-owned media has been decentralised and become available to ordinary citizens. The erstwhile information monopoly was challenged as citizens advanced their own narratives through user-generated social media platforms. For example, this enabled marginalised communities to employ social media to coordinate, facilitate and conduct demonstrations. The Occupy movement, Spain's Indignados and the Arab Spring are among some of the well-known uprisings facilitated through social media.

Due to its closed media systems and repressive political leadership, the Middle East and North Africa (MENA) region bears many similarities with Eritrea. Therefore, I will focus on the Arab Spring for the literature review in order to draw parallels.

As Mohamed Zayani (2016) broadly discusses, the MENA region is best characterised by authoritarian political systems, regional rivalries, conflicting state interests and very closed media systems. A rich investment in media and information technology was mainly manifested in wide penetration of satellite TV stations across the region. With the exception of Al Jazeera, as most media outlets, particularly satellite TV stations, were either state-owned or owned by interest groups that benefit from the status quo, they provided few alternative voices (pp.23–24).

What was singularly missing in traditional media and other public forums made a blazing return with the advent of social media. Rightly, social media has been credited with creating increased interconnectedness and strengthening national and regional identities. As Chebib and Sohail (2011) argue, the increased social ties and real-time information exchange, bypassing traditional channels of communication in the MENA region, have pushed individuals to take action. In a region that long suffered from extreme centralisation of information and ubiquitous censorship, social media sites opened radical new possibilities. Anonymity and horizontal communication were two vital assets that helped social media activists build confidence and stay relatively safe from state arrest.

Miller (2017) argues that apart from accessing information, social media has helped to create social harmony and strengthen relationships between citizens who have been ignored by their leaders. Therefore, the author stipulates, it helped them build trust, discuss at liberty challenges they had been facing, and raise awareness of social injustice. Miller maintains that social media has emerged as the main challenger to the state in the MENA countries as a result of three distinct characteristics. First, they shifted the old analogue 'one-to-many' top-down communication model to a 'many-to-many' interactive model. In societies where the population had been subjected to tedious state-led access to information, Miller argued, the new model created immediate horizontal solidarity (p.252).

In addition to challenging the traditional communication model, the ease of production and distribution of information provided by social media sites played a big role. As Miller (2017) discusses, this new opportunity challenged the hegemonic control of the state and media corporations. Although this applies equally in democratic countries with free and independent media, in the case of MENA, whose states enjoyed a complete information monopoly, activists leapt at the opportunities offered by this new media.

Theoretical framework

My paper draws three theoretical arguments from public sphere theory, speaking truth to power and social media as disruptors.

Public sphere theory is formulated by Jürgen Habermas (original 1962; 1991) in which private citizens come together in public places to discuss issues of common concern over the governing body. Social media activists by their nature are concerned private citizens who come together to discuss issues of great public interest. The fact that Habermas's public sphere is conceived by concerned citizens built along horizontal lines of information flow, as opposed to a top-down state/corporation cantered approach, fits into my theoretical argument.

My paper will draw some theoretical underpinning from Foucault's idea of *parrhesia,* speaking truth to power (Pearson, 2001). Social media activists resort to their particular communication platform as a means of challenging the repressive regimes because they otherwise lack free access and protection.

Challenging the information blockage and status quo through decentred mechanisms is another important angle of my paper. This is what Hardt and Negri also proposed in their *Declaration* (2012). Before even attempting to establish a system, social media activists strive to dismantle the existing structure of the repressive regimes. Therefore, in addition to the two broader theoretical underpinnings, I will borrow the disruptive aspect from Hardt and Negri.

Contributions of social media in Eritrea

For most locals inside the country, accessing even the slow internet connection is unbearable as citizens depend on crowded and public internet cafes, making it difficult to access 'unfavourable' content. Despite all the difficulties in Eritrea, the tech-savvy youth population is connected to the outside with other communication channels such as the widely available satellite dishes and family members in the diaspora. Tired of the prolonged sufferings, it is natural that such a population would look for any alternative sources to defy the state imposition. Eritreans living inside the country are not totally disconnected with the events outside. Media outlets such as Radio Erena, Radio Assenna, VOA and BBC Tigrinya or websites like Awate, Asmarino and Assenna are very popular and considered as the most reliable sources of information on Eritrea. The media outlets accessed inside Eritrea serve as a bridge between the two populations and amplify messages that circulate on Eritrean social media. At the receiving end, in Eritrea, this is met with a very communal culture where most youth frequent public spaces to hang out and stay in touch. News posted on any opposition sites is widely discussed and shared in the cafes.

I will discuss some of the significant contributions of social media. I will provide examples when necessary.

Some of the established mechanisms that enabled the Eritrean regime to continue its rule were: secrecy; instilling fear and mistrust; and overall creating the impression that PFDJ is capable of silencing anyone even after fleeing the country. Social media has broken this tradition and helped many Eritreans conquer their fear and demystify the power of the regime. The first step was exposing its vulnerability to dismantle the 'indomitable' leaders. Thanks to the different platforms, many have come out to speak openly using their real identities. This serves double in cultivating accountability and responsibility which were largely missing in the Eritrean political culture.

Due to the nature of the ruling system and limited access, although it might not serve as a full record, social media sites have helped document the horrendous abuses committed by the ruling party. As members of the team who have been interviewed for this research argue, during the investigation by the UN Commission Inquiry on Human Rights in Eritrea, social media played a vital role in connecting and reporting to the Commission.

Social media sites did not only help document the crimes committed, but also assisted in identifying key perpetrators of crimes. Thanks to the wide sharing of information, corroborated with different accounts, individuals who continue to cause harm have been identified. In a closed society like Eritrea, what has been shared and discussed on social media sites quickly reaches Eritrea and serves as a watchdog. When officials are identified by name in unfavourable reports, former government employees who were close to the key post tell that it causes them panic.

Information flow has been strictly one-way and the Eritrean government has long enjoyed an information monopoly. Communication between the huge diaspora community and family members in Eritrea has been reduced to the bare minimum as most do not feel safe to speak openly about anything considered a sensitive subject. Despite such imposition, crucial information that would later reach the international media has been leaked or broken via social media. Afterwards, the independent media pick stories from social media sites to amplify it. There are many examples that were initially leaked through the social media that have major impact.

In April 2016, some national service members who were escorted to the Assab front after finishing their military training jumped out of their trucks and attempted to escape. When the soldiers opened fire and killed some of those who had attempted to flee, including bystanders, the incident was captured by mobile phone, sent to some contacts outside and quickly circulated on social media. As there was documented evidence, the state could not deny it as it would have been with others. Other significant documentation was the 2016 hidden camera of Ethiopia-based Radio Wegahta. As it was widely circulated on social media, the video – that was later used in different documentaries on Eritrea – captured the horrendous situation of Eritrean prison centres. The October 2017 Akria demonstration was able to get media traction thanks to the wide sharing of videos though social media. Starting from the impassioned speech of Haji Mussa Mohammednur to the later demonstration that was met with gunfire to the protest later in the funeral procession, all were captured with smartphone and leaked to the diaspora community. Then it was quickly picked by the West's mainstream media and gained international coverage (Al Jazeera, 2017). Other breaking news that reached a wider audience through social media included the December 2018 assassination attempt of General Sebhat Ephrem.

More than breaking the news cycle, as many social media activists argue, with all its challenges social media continues to serve as the main most reliable platform to discuss events and act on follow-ups. Especially, the Live Facebook feature has opened an opportunity where an engaged citizen would respond to new developments in Eritrea. These open forums help shape the discourse, create awareness, garner support for some causes and later contribute through different means, from crowdfunds to signing petitions to demonstrations.

Social media has enabled many young potential leaders to assert their readiness as potential community leaders and organisers. Bypassing the traditional structures of authority, many young men and women are emerging and claiming ownership of their own affairs. In the absence of civic society and other public platforms, it won't have been easy to tell who is who in the widely scattered Eritrean diaspora community.

Eritrean youth have been denied of agency over the last two decades. When the youth were fleeing in thousands, trekking the deadly Mediterranean Sea and Sahara Desert in search of safety, the majority depended on communication and information sharing via social media. Many have fallen prey to human traffickers in exchange for huge ransoms. As the state failed to take responsibility, many are taking the matter in hand to help the destitute Eritrean refugees through crowdfunding, demonstrations (as in the case of Libya) and amplifying their plights through social media to reach leading international media. Social media continues to play a crucial role, even after the destitute refugees are freed from captivity. Navigating the asylum processes, coping mechanisms in each country and overall support is mostly reduced to social media. Some might argue that refugees do not have a role in challenging the repressive regime in Eritrea, but it is only after they have settled that they can start to fight back against the oppressor. Social media helps many to build confidence and then reflect their arduous journey. As many were conditioned to that repressive lifestyle for their entire lives, they only realised the difference and reflected in retrospect when others started to speak out and share their plights. The process helps many to examine themselves and clearly see where the fault lies.

While these are some of the significant contributions of social media on the general level, some deserve special attention. One of these is a Facebook page called Sactism/Sacttism.

The role of Facebook page 'Sacttism'

A popular Facebook page called 'Sacttism: Classified Documents of Dwindling PFDJ' was founded by an anonymous whistle-blower in February 2016. Although it is very difficult to verify all the claims made by the page, other independent sources have corroborated the claims posted on the page. The page, now inactive since June 2018, has published many pieces of crucial information and exposed some of the alleged crimes committed at the hands of the regime. Among others were the conditions of the political prisoners and journalists who have been kept captive since September 2001. In a series of posts, the page detailed the conditions, responsible individuals and conditions of each prisoner. Prior to the posts on the page, no such detailed accounts on conditions and the responsible individuals had been made public. The page widely documented and had provided updates on most crucial issues, garnering a weekly average readership of between 250,000 and 350,000 hits. According to information relayed by the page admin, at times it reached a hit rate of 700,000 per week (Zere, 2016a).

Apart from providing detailed information on different subjects and incidents, the page was used to share alleged documents to substantiate the claims. By doing so it was quickly established as a most reliable source. For example, in February 2017 the page announced that former Minister of Foreign Affairs, Haile 'Durue' Woldensae died in custody. The post garnered around 2,000 shares and a thread of comment that reached 4,500 in just a couple of days (Zere, 2018a). Whether the news could be verified or not, it served as a wake up call for the Eritrean community to come together and reignite the struggle for justice.

Overall, despite the continued hostilities by the regime, the page Sacttism served as a most crucial opponent by continuously publishing classified materials allegedly accessed from inside Eritrea. Posts on the page were widely shared on different platforms and read by radio stations such as Assenna that reach Eritrea.

So far, I have been mainly discussing the role of social media in pressuring the repressive regime among the Eritrean diaspora community. But there is no doubt that a real lasting change should come from inside the country. It is important to measure its effects inside Eritrea. The next section will attempt to see this aspect.

Social media's spiral effect inside Eritrea

Despite the heavy state imposition, Eritreans inside the country have devised their own ways of staying in touch with the outside world. As sources from inside the country or others who have recently left the country attest, critical posts on Eritrea would be downloaded in offices that have faster internet access and then be widely read and shared via USB flash disks. Internet cafes have turned into hubs of sharing music videos, films and other 'unfavourable materials' due to the slow internet connection (Zere, 2018b).

Apart from the risky task of sharing resources, social media has influenced Eritrean politics by shaping the music industry. The Eritrean regime established itself, among other means, by using vicious propaganda enabled through the arts and media. The emergence of the Eritrean owned YouTube channels has effectively changed the established tradition of disproportionate patriotic songs. Before the popularity of YouTube music, even those who had different political stances had to depend on the propaganda-driven music industry of the state media. Now both producers and singers must work to produce content that appeals to a free audience, effectively ending the monotonous praise songs that long dominated the Eritrean music industry. The YouTube industry dismantles the government's authority to select which musicians get coverage.

The online music industry has its own checks and balances. If singers slightly slip from what is expected and side with the regime, the response is instant. For example, in August 2017 when the singer Eseyas Debesay teamed up with the Yohannes sisters, who were enjoying fame, to produce a song that mocked the youth who are leaving the country, the response was quick. Within a week the clip accumulated more than 30,000 dislikes and a thread of comments that stretched to about 7,000 mostly calling for a boycott of the artists (Zere, 2018b). Despite their talents and many appealing songs after that, the Yohannes sisters were unable to come back. The same has happened to the legendary singer Asghedom W. Michael after composing a praise song at a time when Eritreans were growing wary of the peace deal. The reaction forced the YouTube channel to disable the like and dislike buttons which later pressured the owner to publicly apologise.

This is a new challenge to the regime that enjoyed the exclusive right of shaping its narrative and had sustained a nation with a deceptive narrative. The online music industry not only spared the propaganda theme songs but garnered many lead singers to join the justice-seekers camp. The majority of the YouTube music consumers are the youth who have recently fled the country. If artists exhibit an ambivalent political position in the ongoing struggle for justice, they risk being boycotted. As a result, many singers who have been silent in fear of displeasing some supporters after fleeing the country have started to openly criticise the regime with their works.

Apart from shaping the music industry, the social media driven resistance has influence on the politics inside Eritrea. After the July 2018 peace deal with Ethiopia, the Eritrean diaspora equipped with social media and the independent media has been operating as an offshore opposition both to check Isaias Afwerki's unhindered single-handed policies and Abiy Ahmed's murky position. The leaders continue to sign hidden deals that would later inadvertently come to the surface. As the Eritrean regime continued for months without disclosing the agreement, Eritreans in the diaspora were able to organise public demonstrations in front of the Ethiopian embassies in London and Washington DC demanding the Ethiopian authorities to respect Eritrean sovereignty. Demonstrators warned that it will have worse consequences if Ethiopian authorities continue to ignore the demand. As some organisers who have been interviewed reveal, such demonstrations and consolidating the wider discontent were enabled through social media. The pressure against the Eritrean regime's total silence has been taken further since mid-February 2019. Social media activists started to challenge each other; record messages on Facebook and other social media platforms calling for an end of silence and rule of law. The challenge went viral and in a short time leading artists, religious leaders and many former silent majorities came out to openly share their concerns. Slowly, from individual posts, this challenge elevated to physical meetings and discussions. The ongoing challenge has broken many barriers and created a sense of hope among the scattered Eritrean diaspora community. The messages have reverberated in Eritrea as they were widely amplified by the diaspora media (Zere, 2019).

For the Eritrean population inside the country that was mostly at odds with the diaspora community as accomplices of the ongoing repression by continuously supporting the regime, such direct communication revives hope. By disregarding the bar imposed by the regime from direct communication between the two parties, such grassroots initiative creates a bridge.

The #Enough challenge and wider calls through social media have effects in Eritrea both on the public and the political leadership. Some attribute public seminars conducted in March in Eritrea after more than eight months of silence to the wider discontent expressed via social media. It might be difficult to conclude that they were in response to the wider social media driven calls for change, yet it is impossible to rule out that the social media calls didn't play a role. As the widely shared concern among the Eritrean diaspora is about Eritrea's national sovereignty, the seminars made sure to address the subject. According to the state news outlets during the seminars, '[The senior government officials] explained, all the deals Eritrea signs with Ethiopia and other regional states recognize the sovereignty of its land and water territories and is based on clear international charters' (Haddas Ertra, 2019). Such an underlying tone is an indirect address to the growing pressure.

While these are some examples, others show how social media has turned into a formidable opposition that needs to be taken seriously and responded to accordingly.

Combining online and offline opposition

The social media driven resistance extends to real activism. In the recent ongoing wide resistance, different communities gathered to discuss possible actions and express their readiness to take part or contribute financially.

Huge turn outs in Geneva 2015 and 2016 have been largely attributed to the social media driven calls. After the release of the report of the UN Commission of Inquiry on Human Rights in Eritrea, an estimated 5,000 and 12,000 Eritreans gathered in Geneva in 2015 and 2016 respectively to express their support for the Commission's findings. Organisers of the demonstration who have been interviewed for the research attribute such huge turn outs to the calls and wide information sharing via social media sites (Zere, 2016b). Such turn outs unsettle the regime that long claimed a strong support of the Eritrean diaspora community. It similarly sends a message of solidarity to Eritreans inside the country.

Other times, the effect of social media activism is evident in public petitions. Through collective petition, in 2016, Eritrean social media activists were able to ban Yemane Gebreab, the political affairs head of the ruling party, from coming to the USA and conducting public seminars (Awate, 2016). Similarly, activists have successfully petitioned to outlaw the 2 per cent Eritrean diaspora tax in many countries of the West (Dahir, 2018).

Upending the regime's long silence

Having effectively closed all independent media, made the internet nearly inaccessible and closed civic society, the Eritrean regime is realising that social media has been the new front in challenging its near total control. This becomes even more severe as they are unable to shape the discourse among their last base of support and lifeline: the Eritrean diaspora community. Locals inside the country have long abandoned the state media as a source of accurate information, which is mutually understood both by the producers and the receivers. Therefore, the primary targets of the state media and its propaganda are supporters outside. As information is being shared widely by other informal channels, which repeatedly prove to be more accurate than the state media's, the regime is heavily investing in social media.

When state media fails to cover significant developments, but reaches the diaspora activists on social media, then the Eritrean Minister of Information habitually responds in a tweet. Such attempts are meant both to downplay the incidents and give supporters talking points on how to justify and counter the inevitable criticism.

For example, in April 2016, members of the national service who were being escorted to Assab after military training jumped from trucks. The guards responded in gunshots killing and injuring some members. The Human Rights Council in its 2016 report stated that a considerable number of conscripts and bystanders (p.32) were killed but was unable to provide exact figures. Independent journalist and researcher, Martin Plaut, based on sources inside the country, claimed that a total of 29 people were killed and injured. Opposition sites such as Assenna.com reported four were killed. Although it was difficult to confirm the exact figures, as some captured the video of shooting and this was widely shared on social media, it was impossible to conceal it. The national media didn't cover the incident. In an attempt to quell the rage, six days after the incident the Eritrean Minister of Information, Yemane G. Meskel, tweeted: 'Eritrea's arch-enemies and hired guns have now gone into their usual frantic-mode to conjure up & recycle despicable lies of a sad incident.' Despite his initial attempt of blaming 'arch-enemies', it was impossible to completely deny it. Then, in a tweet, he stated, 'Two National Service members died last Sunday in Asmara from injuries received when they jumped & fell from military trucks transporting them' and added that 11 others were injured. The minister didn't mention the shooting in his tweet.

Another example is the case of Akria's demonstration. On 31 October 2018, when the students and parents of Al Diaa Islamic School came out to demonstrate and ask for the release of the school parents' president, they were met with gunfire. Videos of the demonstration and the speech of Haji Mussa Mohammednur, who later died in custody, were widely circulated and were picked up by leading international media outlets. As this went out of control, the Minister of Information had to chime in to downplay the incident: 'Small demonstration by one school in Asmara dispersed without any causality (sic) hardly breaking news', he tweeted.

Occasionally, other state officials help the Minister of Information to tweet statements that would serve as the official statement of the government with the same aim of addressing supporters in the diaspora. The assassination attempt of General Sebhat Ephrem that happened on 19 December 2018 went viral on social media the next morning. Three days after the incident the Eritrean ambassador to Japan tweeted and wished the minister a quick recovery.

The investment on social media, however, is not limited to the tweets of senior government officials. As credible sources have relayed, there is a social media team that was initially formulated by the head of Political Affairs of PFDJ, Yemane Gebreab. Members of the group include local college/university graduates and diaspora returnees or interns to tackle social media in non-Eritrean languages, particularly on Twitter. Among other activities, such as trolling and promoting posts that paint a rosy picture of Eritrea, some members of the group were also running a Facebook page called Hagerawi Dihnet (National Security). Until it was deactivated in March 2019, the page was at the forefront of disseminating rumours of possible tips from top state officials.

Among the tech-savvy diaspora supporters, the weight given to social media and its investment is heavier. The Young People's Front for Democracy and Justice (YPFDJ), the protege of the ruling party, receive seminars on how to fight social media. As some members who have attended some of the seminars relayed, training includes talking points on counter-attack. Such seminars identify key opponents that need to be silenced and trolled on social media where their handles and social media accounts would be discussed and identified.

Outcomes of such coordinated trolling attacks are evident. Many vocal critics have been viciously attacked via social media platforms and the regime-friendly websites. This might reach death threats (Shearlaw, 2015). Occasionally, this goes further, as in the case of the popular Facebook page called Sacttism, which was banned twice by Facebook after it received petitions claiming that the page was inciting hatred. As the page was exclusively publishing in Tigrinya, it was impossible for the Facebook team to verify the content and confirm if the claim was true (Zere, 2016a). As I can attest from my personal experience, my blog was attacked by a malware virus on 21 March 2018 and was put down for a day until I was able to recover it a day later. The attack happened after I posted an article in Tigrinya in response to an interview aired in the state media. In an attempt to limit the article's readership via social media, probably the same people have reported the article to Facebook. An attempt to post the article on Facebook declines with a message stating that it goes against their 'community standards' and cannot be accessed.

Different examples as given above show the level of seriousness with which the regime is handling the new social media frontier. As there are no other reliable mechanisms that measure the effectiveness of the social media-driven movements in challenging the Eritrean regime, such reactions provide a glimpse.

Coping with the flaws of social media platforms

Social media sites are criticised as enablers of rumours and spreaders of unverified news. Such challenge doubles in cases like Eritrea where information is tightly controlled, sifted and only distributed in a way to benefit the regime. As a result, the Eritrean diaspora community has been prey to false information. Some news might be proven to be rumours long after creating excitement or panic.

Over time it seems this flaw is self-correcting, at least to minimise damage. Many active social media users have established credibility as reliable sources or candid analysts with better insights. As a result, many are now checking the source before sharing. Others are emerging as sound and reasonable analysts in the widely available social media platforms such as Facebook and YouTube channels. Therefore, those who have established names are filling the gap and serve as grassroots independent media in their capacities.

The shift of narrative on social media

In times where most meaningful conversations are taking place on social media, who controls the platform controls the narrative. For Eritreans who have been left without agents, taking control of the thinking space is unparalleled. Among other platforms, Twitter has been dominated by the regime supporters for a long time. The main reason for this could be due to the regime's coordinated effort to dominate the platform and the fact that the majority of its supporters are the diaspora-born Eritreans who are better equipped with the language most of the international community understands.

But this seems to have shifted recently. A few Eritrean state officials who extensively use the platform are facing new challenges, this time with nationals who use their real names and disclose their identities. Unable to cope with the new challenge, state officials such as the Minister of Information, Eritrean ambassador to Japan, Kenya and others are quickly resorting to blocking. Prior to that the fear of imperilling family members back home and the fact that many Eritrean activists were not using Twitter had enabled them to spread their propaganda unchallenged.

The second reason for the shifting of Twitter domination is because justice seekers started to take coordinated and proactive measures. As I was able to access it, some social media activists are taking the initiative to create informal networks to strategise their efforts and send coordinated messages. Among others, the #Enough/#Yiakl challenge that later went viral and took over other platforms was initiated by such a group.

For the regime supporters who have long enjoyed the platform and managed to silence activists through coordinated trolling, the new reality was hard to accept. For example, Simon Tesfamariam, handle name @RedSeaFisher, who is reportedly one of the organisers of the social media counter offense, tweeted on 13 March 2019 that Twitter is shadow banning pro-government tweets (Tesfamariam, 2019). This is an indication that justice seekers are taking ownership of Twitter. Apart from that, a cursory search for #Eritrea easily shows the shift of posts.

Challenges of social media driven activism

Despite all the factors listed as liberating examples, it would be a mistake to continue without discussing some of the challenges posed through social media. Some are attributed to the nature of the social media sites while others might be more prevalent in the Eritrean context.

Scholars of networking societies (Barnett, 2011; Skoric and Zhu, 2016) argue that the increase in digital communication and social network sites decreases physical participation. Especially as the Eritrean diaspora has only the leverage of pressuring from afar and exposing the crimes of the regime, the digital activism has obvious limitations in securing real change on the ground.

Social media sites increase political polarisation through selective exposure and creating echo-chambers (Shanini-Hoxhaj, 2018; Lee and Hahn, 2018). This further exacerbates the already polarised Eritrean population. When everyone is framed in the rubric of 'supporters' and 'opposition' labels, attacks become personal, which quickly trickles down to family members and friends as in a small community. Therefore, we do not often observe activists changing camps and openly declaring their stance or genuinely acknowledging that they have been wrong. The farthest one camp can go is to stop being vocal and keep silent. Due to this, social media has the potential to help the silent majority voice their disenchantments, but does not necessarily play a favourable role in converting the opposing camp.

The long impasse of the political atmosphere inside Eritrea has waned many activists. Over its long course activists who were unable to effectively challenge the autocratic regime inside Eritrea have turned to their fellow activists in the same camp. Expectedly, the Eritrean state security or other forces such as Ethiopian security apparatus with different agenda have played a negative role using social media to tarnish the credibility of activists. This contributes to cultivating a culture of cynicism and a lack of trust.

Social media sites have been criticised as enablers of populism and the rise of right-wing political leaders in the West. Examples of such were witnessed during the Brexit referendum in the UK and the election of Donald Trump in the USA (Khosravinik, 2017; Engesser, Ernst, Esser and Büchel, 2017). This too had left its mark on Eritrean social media. Before reaching their final destinations, the majority of the recently immigrated Eritreans have gone through arduous journeys in the Sahara and the Mediterranean Sea. As the journey is best characterised as survival of the fittest, over the course of their journey many have been bitter about others. This led to further divisions along religious and sub-regional lines in which many had no option but to stick what best became a safety net. When social media opened a 'free' platform for the traumatised youth, many quickly went to attacks which led to fermenting sub-national and regional or religious sentiments. The highest epitome of this was manifested in some of the odd and critically dangerous trends such as the Agazian movement (Yehuda, 2018). Such were easily manipulated by other regional political actors such as Ethiopia to serve their agenda.

Social media by their own nature are prone to spreading fake news with greater potential to cause panic. Such a trait is doubly challenging in the case of Eritrea as it is nearly impossible to verify rumours. Apart from self-correcting by other users, it has become difficult to counter and verify unfounded claims.

As I am mainly dealing with the political aspect, I am not giving enough emphasis to the widely argued negative consequences of social media, particularly in the developed world. As has been widely documented by various leading scholars, social media sites by nature are prone to bullying, the tyranny of majority and too much noise, where average readers can't discern accurate facts from false or misleading claims (Hogan, 2011; Tarwani, Chrasia and Shukla, 2017). These may be widely reflected when the populace has other options for accessing and sharing information. In such cases social media becomes an option, but not a necessity, as in the case of Eritrea.

A way forward?

Eritreans have resorted to social media as their main outlet because of a lack of established traditional media. In the process, the 'alternative' media has taken over the mainstream media. The ultimate solution is creating formidable and authentic media, but meanwhile there are some ways of best utilisation of social media with the ongoing crisis. As long as social media serves as the main option for cracking the information blockage, there are some aspects that the Eritrean diaspora can take for a better use:

- There is a need for greater media literacy where citizens would be able to discern false claims by cultivating critical scrutiny and identifying sources.

- Despite all the challenges in order to avoid tarnishing their credibility, the diaspora-based independent Eritrean media outlets need to take extra steps to verify and use their judgement before disseminating the news. This is crucial at this juncture because the state security can deliberately feed tips that can later discredit the media outlets in the eyes of the wider audience.

- Although it might not always be easy, social media users are advised to identify users who often spread unfounded rumours and others with solid credibility. If possible, it is also better to triangulate the information before sharing it.

- Instead of only depending on excerpts from quotes, it is always advised to check the source.

References

Yemane Gebreab, number 7, can't host meetings in the US, Awate.com (2 October 2016) http://awate.com/yemane-gebreab-number-7-cant-host-meetings-in-the-us/

Barnett, M. Empire of Humanity: A History of Humanitarianism (Ithaca and London: Cornell University Press, 2011).

Chebib, N. and Sohail, R.M. 'The reasons social media contributed to the 2011 Egyptian revolution' (2011) 2(2) International Journal of Business Research and Management 139–62.

10 Most Censored Countries, Committee to Protect Journalists (2015) https://cpj.org/2015/04/10-most-censored-countries.php

Dahir, A.L. The Netherlands has expelled Eritrea's top diplomat for forcing Eritreans to pay a 'diaspora tax', Quartz Africa (19 January 2018) https://qz.com/africa/1183766/netherlands-expels-eritreas-top-diplomat-for-diaspora-tax/

Engesser, S., Ernst, N.S., Esser, F. and Büchel, F. 'Populism and social media: how politicians spread a fragmented ideology' (2017) 20(8) Information, Communication & Society 1109–26.

Fairclough, N. Discourse and Social Change. (Harlow: Pearson Education, 1992).

Gagliardone, I. and Stremlau, N. Digital media, conflict and diasporas in the Horn of Africa, Open Society Foundations (2011).

Gebremeskel, Y. [Hawelti] (8 April 2016) Eritrea's arch-enemies and hired guns have now gone into their usual frantic-mode to conjure up & recycle despicable lies of a sad incident. [Tweet]. Retrieved from https://twitter.com/hawelti/status/718415711958392833

Gebremeskel, Y. [Hawelti] (8 April 2016). Two National Service members died last Sunday in Asmara from injuries received when they jumped & fell from military trucks transporting them. [Tweet]. Retrieved from https://twitter.com/hawelti/status/718412866685116416

Gebremeskel, Y. [Hawelti] (8 April 2016). 11 others were also injured in the same act & have been hospitalized. Police stabilized z situation by firing few warning shots into z air. [Tweet]. Retrieved from https://twitter.com/hawelti/status/718415299146551296

Gebremeskel, Y. [Hawelti] (31 October 2017). Plaut is a pathological liar par excellence. Small demonstration by one school in Asmara dispersed without any casuality hardly breaking news. [Tweet]. Retrieved from https://twitter.com/hawelti/status/925451372581015552

Habermas, J. The Structural Transformation of the Public Sphere: An Inquiry into a Category Of Bourgeois Society (Habermas, J. and McCarthy, T., trans.) (Cambridge, MA: MIT Press, 1991; original work published 1962).

Hardt, M. and Negri, A. Declaration (Argo-Navis, 2012).

Hogan, P. 'Your brain on new media: communicative democracy, tyranny, and enabling ambivalence' (2011) 4(1) Theory in Action 48–69.

Howard, P. and Hussain, M. 'The role of digital media' (2011) 22(3) Journal of Democracy 35–48.

Khosravinik, M. 'Right wing populism in the West: social media discourse and echo chambers' (2017) 19(3) Insight Turkey 53–68.

Lee, H. and Hahn, K.S. 'Partisan selective following on twitter over time: polarization or depolarization?' (2018) 28(3) Asian Journal of Communication 227–46.

Miller, V. 'Phatic culture and the status quo: Reconsidering the purpose of social media activism' (2017) 23(3) Convergence 251–69.

Pearson, J. Michel Foucault: Fearless Speech (Los Angeles: Semiotext(e), 2001).

Plaut, M. Eritrea: naming the dead and injured conscripts in Asmara shooting, Martinplaut.wordpress (7 April 2016) https://martinplaut.wordpress.com/2016/04/07/eritrea-naming-the-dead-and-injured-conscripts-in-asmara-shooting/

World press freedom index 2017, Reporters Without Borders (2017) https://rsf.org/en/ranking/2017

World press freedom index 2018, Reporters Without Borders (2018) https://rsf.org/en/ranking/2018

Shanini-Hoxahaj, R. 'Facebook and political polarization: an analysis of the social media impact on the Kosovo-Serbia dialogue' (2018) 11(3) Journal of Media Research 71–93.

Shearlaw, M. From online trolling to death threats – the war to defend Eritrea's reputation, The Guardian (18 August 2015) https://www.theguardian.com/world/2015/aug/18/eritrea-death-threats-tolls-united-nations-social-media

Skoric, M.M. and Zhu, Q. 'Social media and offline political participation: uncovering the paths from digital to physical' (2016) 28(3) International Journal of Public Opinion Research 415–27.

Tarwani, N., Chorasia, U. and Shukla, P.K. 'Survey of cyberbullying detection on social media big-data' (2017) 8(5) International Journal of Advanced Research in Computer Science 831–35.

Tesfamarim, S. [RedSeaFisher] (13 March 2019) Twitter is shadow banning Eritrean nationalist and government tweets, which regularly receive 100+ retweets, in favor of unpopular regime-change activist tweet, which barely muster 30 (mostly from cronies/NGOs). Twitter helps them make up for their unpopularity. #DigitalWeyane. [Tweet]. Retrieved from https://twitter.com/search?q=Twitter%20is%20shadow%20banning%20Eritrean&src=typd

Tronvoll, K. The Lasting Struggle for Freedom in Eritrea: Human Rights and Political Development, 1991–2009. (Oslo: Oslo Center for Peace and Human Rights, 2009).

Internet usage and population stats in Africa, World Internet Stats (2019) https://www.internetworldstats.com/africa.htm#er

Zayani, M. 'On the entangled questions of media and politics in the Middle East', in Zayani, M. and Mirgani, S. (eds) Bullets and Bulletins: Media and Politics in the Wake of the Arab Uprisings (Oxford: Oxford University Press, 2016) pp.23–43.

Yehuda, I.B. The far-right nationalist movement roiling Eritreans in Israel, +972Mag (7 May 2018) https://972mag.com/the-far-right-nationalist-movement-roiling-eritreans-in-israel/135179/

Zere, A.T. Facebook page vows to lift the lid on Eritrea's secret reign of terror, The Guardian (27 April 2016a) https://www.theguardian.com/world/2016/apr/27/eritrea-facebook-page-sactism-human-rights-abuses

Zere, A.T. Eritrea: An exiled nation suspended in liminal space through the social media, Carnegie Council of Ethics in International Affairs (30 December 2016) https://www.carnegiecouncil.org/publications/ethics_online/0125

Zere, A.T. Remembering the day the Eritrean press died, Al Jazeera English (18 September 2017) https://www.aljazeera.com/indepth/opinion/remembering-day-eritrean-press-died-170918074330130.html

Zere, A.T. The Eritrean diaspora is mourning, Al Jazeera English (21 March 2018a) https://www.aljazeera.com/indepth/opinion/eritrean-diaspora-mourning-180301114427157.html

Zere, A.T. Whatever happened to Afwerki's comely face? Eritrean music in an age of YouTube, African Arguments (13 February 2018b) https://africanarguments.org/2018/02/13/whatever-happened-to-afwerkis-comely-face-eritrea-music-in-an-age-of-youtube/

Zere, A.T. The Eritrean Diaspora is Unsettling its Autocratic Regime Through Social Media, Toward Freedom (9 April 2019)

Martin Plaut

Journalist, author and senior research fellow, Institute of Commonwealth Studies, University of London

Eritrea and the international media – a way forward

The context

It is a familiar problem. The coverage provided by the international media of Eritrea is sketchy, at best. On 28 March 2019 (one day, taken at random) the best the media could offer were stories on Eritrean cycling (always a good story, and true of course),[136] a report that surface-to-air missiles bound for Eritrea had been unearthed in Ukraine[137] and an uninformative story about an Eritrean delegation in Japan.[138] By comparison, the coverage of Ethiopia was far more serious. There were, of course, a good number of articles about the Ethiopian air crash and the Boeing 373's safety,[139] which was of international concern. But there were also really serious assessments of Ethiopian politics in the *Financial Times*,[140] a careful analysis of the Ethiopian economy[141] and the country's relations with China[142] and the USA.[143]

This is a pattern Eritreans are very familiar with. Their country is seldom covered by the international media while other countries in the Horn of Africa like Ethiopia and Somalia attract a fair amount of journalistic attention. There are a variety of reasons for this. For a start, it is difficult to get into Eritrea. The country only rarely issues visas for the media. It does not allow any reputable media house (Reuters, BBC, Al Jazeera, etc.) to have a permanent presence in the country and controls the travel and reporting of visiting journalists very tightly. As a result, all visits by visiting media tend to report on familiar topics: Asmara as a beautiful art-deco city; the passion for cycling; the potential for tourism on the coast; the archaeology and wildlife. All these topics have been covered repeatedly in the past. No independent Eritrean media activity is allowed inside the country that might alert foreign reports to interesting stories. On top of this Eritrea is at peace (so why report from there?), has few economic issues to report on (apart from two mining projects) and the repression is carefully hidden away. As a result, there are few international editors willing to send their correspondents on the long, expensive journey and coverage of Eritrea is sketchy at best.

What can be done?

It is important to look ahead and not see this as an insuperable problem. Any action is better than none; all action should begin with some study and analysis of what the obstacles and possibilities really are.

1. Monitor international coverage

Eritrea Focus and the Europe External Policy Advisors (EEPA) already do this. Together they would provide an even more useful source. Could we add an American and perhaps an Israeli and an African contact? We could all post on each other's websites to provide a united, comprehensive source of information that everyone could draw on. It would not rule out separate organisations circulating targeted, less comprehensive information.

2. Get to know who writes internationally

There are a relatively small number of reporters who serve the international media from the Horn of Africa. People like Tom Gardner, who writes for the *Economist* and *Guardian* is one, but there are others. There are others who write on the Horn of Africa from London, Paris and Washington.

We could, together, construct a single list and gradually add contact details which we might all share. This would require a degree of trust, since we should be careful not to bombard them with information, but it should not be impossible.

3. Specialist journalism

There are a range of specialist publications which might be seen as 'feeders' of the international media. For example, mining magazines and news sources are picked up and used by mainstream journalists wishing to cover the region.

136   https://www.bbc.co.uk/news/world-africa-47709673
137   https://www.janes.com/article/87516/ukraine-says-it-found-russian-sams-destined-for-eritrea
138   https://www.africanews.com/2019/03/28/japan-eritrea-foreign-ministers-meeting-and-working-lunch/
139   https://qz.com/africa/1580369/ethiopian-airlines-may-not-attend-boeing-737-max-crash-meeting/
140   https://www.ft.com/content/1cbaac04-457f-11e9-a965-23d669740bfb
141   https://www.brookings.edu/blog/africa-in-focus/2019/03/26/ethiopia-africas-next-powerhouse/
142   https://www.theafricareport.com/11080/ethiopias-china-challenge/
143   https://www.africanews.com/2018/07/26/united-states-expresses-concern-over-prevailing-insecurity-within-ethiopia/

The same could be said of media that specialise in agriculture, ecology or culture. Each hold possibilities for placing stories that relate to their interests.

4. African media outlets

There are a range of international media outlets that specialise in coverage of the Horn of Africa. These include the BBC and VOA African Services, Al Jazeera as well as a range of African magazines. The French and German international radio stations are also always on the lookout for good stories to cover. Again, it is a question of developing contacts and working out who is really working on the area.

5. Make the news

Another demonstration outside the Eritrean embassy is useful for Eritrean media sites – it is not something journalists will cover unless you can get tens of thousands to bring the area to a halt. News is what you didn't know before you heard it. Doing something for a second time is just repetition and not newsworthy. Sadly, yet another drowning in the Mediterranean is a tragedy, but it is not news any more.

All that is required is imagination. Vanessa Berhe has shown what can be done. In September 2018 she staged a 17-minute silent protest for Eritrea to commemorate 17 years since the Eritrean media was closed down and its journalists imprisoned.[144]

So, what is needed is something different. Is there something going on inside the Eritrean community where you live that is really innovative? Let me give a few examples.

I know there was once a very small Jewish Community in Eritrea. Can you track down someone who is a member of this tiny group? Do they have photographs and memories to share? Their story and their history would probably be of interest to the Jewish newspapers.

To take a possible British angle, might it be possible for Eritrea's religious groups to come together to arrange a meeting with one of the Bishops who represent all religions in the House of Lords? This would make news in the Christian press.

Eritrean cycling is a big story for the cycling world. Is there a visiting Eritrean team member who you could help them meet?

6. Personality led coverage

There are many personalities in the world of film, TV and acting who are concerned about atrocities in the developing world. Why not Eritrea? It is a question of seeing who is living in your area and trying to meet them to see if they might be prepared to help get the story across. They can be a useful catalyst.

7. Suggest Eritrea or Eritrean issues in local radio; letters to newspapers, etc.

There is a huge appetite for news in local radio and local newspapers. Don't always think nationally. But you do need a local angle. For example: why not get a group of Eritreans to make a traditional meal for homeless or hungry people in your area? This would give them a meal and allow you to talk about the flight of Eritreans from their own homes and how this has left them homeless – you understand what local people are suffering. Invite the local press, or take photographs and send in a letter with pictures.

8. Use your local organisations, e.g. political party, trade union or student organisation

You are lucky to live in democracies. Politicians and other organisations are open to be worked with and joined. If you support them you can call on them to support your cause. What are you waiting for?

Taking this strategy forward

If this is a way forward then what is required is a small group of people who are willing to commit time to this strategy. Each should represent an area or country and be prepared to put in some time and energy to raise Eritrean issues up the agenda. It can be done, it just requires some time and energy – and a willingness to collaborate and cooperate.

---

144   https://edition.cnn.com/2018/09/19/opinions/eritrea-silent-protest-africa/.

11. Engaging with international democracies

John Stauffer

President, America Team for Displaced Eritreans

The America Team for Displaced Eritreans (AT) is an all-volunteer humanitarian organisation, based near Philadelphia, Pennsylvania, USA, that assists Eritrean refugees and asylum seekers in the USA and around the world. We also advocate for the advancement of human rights within Eritrea.

The AT began its work on behalf of Eritreans in 2003. In 2010 we legally incorporated as a non-profit organisation, at which time we undertook our current mission. Our co-founder and president, John Stauffer, had served as a teacher in the US Peace Corps in Eritrea in the 1960s, when that country was part of Ethiopia. After a long corporate career, by 2006 John had once again become active with Eritrean matters full-time.

Our core group of activists is very small – some were born in Eritrea, and some are American-born non-Eritreans. We receive only private donations and no public funds or government grants. We are not financially compensated for our work.

What we do

1. Assist in individual Eritrean asylum cases in the USA. We do not serve as asylum seekers' legal representatives. Rather, we often are able to:
    *   Help them find lawyers.
    *   Provide them or their lawyers with affidavits and materials on Eritrean country conditions.
    *   Provide interpreting and translating resources.
    *   Help connect them with friends and relatives who can offer support and/or serve as their sponsors should they be paroled or otherwise released from detention.
    *   Provide small stipends for telephone calls during their detention and for transportation upon their release from detention.
    *   Provide sundry other assistance.

2. Assist individual Eritrean refugees who are imperilled overseas. We frequently receive calls from Eritreans who are detained, stranded, in hiding or destitute overseas. We then seek to connect them with NGOs and intergovernmental organisations that can provide them with security, and we occasionally provide them with emergency financial assistance.

3. Assist individual Eritrean refugees who have been resettled in Pennsylvania through the United Nations/ US State Department resettlement process. In limited cases we provide ongoing personal mentoring and support for individuals and families in our geographical area.

4. Raise awareness about Eritrean human rights and refugee issues. We maintain a website that tells the story of Eritrea and Eritrean refugees. The site also contains a library of news items and reference materials; tools helpful to Eritreans who are newly arrived in the United States; and occasional action alerts for grassroots congressional advocacy. We have also worked with many news reporters, have participated in many conferences and have spoken with many other NGOs about the nature and urgency of our work. We helped produce a documentary video about the plight of Eritrean refugees and about their lives in Ethiopian refugee camps and in Israel.

5. Partner with other NGOs, activists, US governmental offices and intergovernmental organisations in their Eritrea-related work. We have been a resource for them with respect to such matters as Eritrean country conditions, the Eritrean refugee community and strategic considerations and we have enjoyed the resources reciprocally offered by them. We have worked with both US and international NGOs and activists. We offer advocacy trainings for Eritrean diaspora groups.

6. Monitor disruptive Eritrean regime activity in the USA. We sometimes gather and report information about activities by the Eritrean regime within the USA that disrupts, interferes with or threatens the lives of Eritrean residents here.

7. Monitor the fairness of US immigration, asylum and removal policies. Those policies may materialise through the operations of both judicial and administrative bodies.

8. Advocate at a policy level. We regularly and privately communicate with US governmental offices in Washington on matters such as Eritrean refugees, asylum seekers, human rights, religious freedom, torture survivors, human trafficking and the hoped-for democratisation of Eritrea. The offices include those of

members of Congress and those of federal administrative agencies. We have led two publicly-released sign-on letters, each of which was co-signed by dozens of other NGOs, large and small. One letter was addressed to US authorities on the subject of threatened forced removals of Eritreans from the USA to Eritrea; and the other was addressed to US and international authorities seeking relief for Eritreans trapped and abused in Libya. We have also testified before the US Congress and have assisted congressional committees in developing agendas for the testimony of others.

Current, critical matters

1. US removal policy. In September 2017, the US government ordered a wholesale removal (deportation) to Eritrea of Eritreans who had been denied asylum by US immigration judges, including some immigration judges who broadly deny asylum to nearly all those who claim it, regardless of the merits. We believe that those Eritreans removed would face certain imprisonment, probable torture and possible execution in Eritrea, and that their removal would violate the Convention Against Torture. We have been intensively contesting the policy both in general and as to particular asylum seekers particularly at risk of removal.

2. Libyan detention centres. We have been intensively seeking to provide security and relief for Eritrean refugees who are being subjected to inhumane treatment in Libyan detention facilities. We have communicated directly with many of the detainees.

3. Ethiopian rapprochement. We have been urging that Eritrea's current rapprochement with Ethiopia not be mistaken for an amelioration of human rights within Eritrea – an amelioration that has generally not occurred. We have also urged that Western democracies hold steadfast to their human rights principles as they pursue closer relations with Eritrea in connection with that rapprochement.

Call for diaspora collaborations

We work extensively with (and our organisation includes) members of the Eritrean diaspora. We would welcome additional collaborations. In particular, our work could benefit immeasurably from diaspora assistance in the following endeavours (asterisked items pertain to US-based assistance only):

1. Interpreting and translating for asylum cases.*
2. Assisting in the resettlement of refugees in local communities.*
3. Data gathering and reporting about the diaspora population in the USA.*
4. Data gathering and reporting about asylum and deportation cases in the USA.*
5. Data gathering and reporting about activities of the Eritrean regime in the USA.*
6. Data gathering and reporting about the most current human rights development within Eritrea.
7. Data gathering and reporting about the circumstances of Eritrean refugees in Ethiopia, Libya, Sudan, Egypt, Israel, Eastern Europe and elsewhere abroad.
8. Advocacy with individual members of the US Congress.*
9. Organisational signatures on sign-on letters directed to governmental and intergovernmental authorities.*

Kristina Melicherova

Kristina Melicherova holds an LLM degree in Human Rights Law from Tilburg University, The Netherlands. She currently works for the Belgium-based organisation as an independent consultant supporting advocacy initiatives focusing on external policies of the EU in the area of migration, refugees, and human trafficking and smuggling. Previously she worked as a junior researcher on dynamics of mixed migration in the Horn of Africa.

There is no peace without people

Since the peace agreement, the European Union has attempted fresh engagement with the Eritrean regime in order to stop migration; however, in this process, they have not engaged with the people of Eritrea. The 11th European Development Funding of €200m for which an agreement was signed in 2016 did not deliver any projects, as the Eritrean government has so far refused to sign any funding agreements. The EU, meanwhile, does not have insight into what the situation is in Eritrea, nor does it have any insight into the peace agreement processes from either Eritrea or Ethiopia. The EU is lacking a head of delegation and, therefore, they do not have the frequent contact that they would like. As a result of this, the EU chose another road to approach the regime.

The European Commission recently announced that it is funding a €20m project in Eritrea to build roads in between Massawa and the Ethiopian border, through the EU Emergency Trust Fund for Africa (ETFA) – the fund's main aim is to address migration crises. To agree on this project, migration commissioner Neven Mimica has discussed and agreed directly with the Eritrean government to start this project in the country. The EU freely admits in its project fiche that national service recruits will be used for building the roads: *'The labour used by the construction companies will consist of three types of personnel: permanent Government professionals; those in national service; and those mobilised from the local community on a cash-for-work basis'* and that *'the costs associated with the actual delivery of the rehabilitation work by the construction companies, including labour costs, will be paid for solely by the Government.'* The Red Sea Trading Corporation (RSTC) will be organising procurement, assisted by UNOPS.

In April 2019, the Foundation for Human Rights for Eritreans, a Netherlands-based organisation of exiled Eritreans, issued the letter of summons to the EU to cease this project immediately. On 1 April, a press conference was held in Brussels during which the representatives of the Foundation and its representing lawyer explained the essentials of the case, in which EEPA was present as observer. The main objective of the legal action is to prevent the EU from financing activities in Eritrea for which forced labour is used. As the letter of summons quotes: 'forced labour will be used in the course of a project which is being financed by the EU. Shockingly, the EU is clearly aware of this and accepts it. The ETFA accepts… that there will be no short-term reforms to the national service.' This is a clear violation of human rights and the EU's adherence to international legal obligations. The letter of summons also states that *'RSTC has been found to engage in the illegal trade of arms in violation of sanctions applicable at that time. The fact the EU willingly and unconditionally pays significant sums of money to such companies is stunning and in violation of the legal obligation of the EU to strengthen human rights.'*

The description and aims of this project show that the attempts of the EU to reduce migration from Eritrea is actually achieving the opposite. The author of this paper has just returned from the Tigray region for research and has observed and confirmed with ARRA officials that around 300 people per day continue to be registered as refugees – around 20–25 per cent of these are national service recruits. The EU is therefore supporting one of the main factors that continues to drive migration and, therefore, human trafficking in countries such as Sudan and Libya. Meanwhile, Eritrea has taken the Chair of the Khartoum Process, the EU-Horn of Africa migration route initiative, despite the evidence of Eritrean authorities' involvement in human trafficking.

The Eritrean diaspora and other organisations have challenged the involvement of the EU and its member states with the Eritrean regime, and other regimes accused of human rights abuses, in recent months. Increasingly, these challenges are taking the form of legal action. For example, in the UK, the Department for International Development (DFID) is being sued for its support to Libya detention centres by an Ethiopian asylum seeker. In addition, the Eritrean regime in the diaspora is also challenged, for example in the Netherlands where, last year, the head of the embassy office was expelled following media per cent reporting on intimidation and threats around the 2% tax and the regret form. It appears, therefore, that rather than just reporting extensively on the issues, legal measures and challenges are the way forward when it comes to the EU's involvement in external action in the Horn of Africa, as well as Eritrea's involvement in Europe through the long arm of the Eritrean regime.

Other events in Brussels in the past months have spotlighted the situation in Eritrea and for Eritrean refugees. The conference : We the People! Peace in the Horn: The Safety and Future of the Eritrean People, from 12 to 14 December 2018, brought together over 200 participants including representatives of Eritrean diaspora, experts, academics, NGOs, politicians and human rights activists. The main objective of the conference was to provide a platform for different stakeholders to share, exchange and learn on the new reality of the peace agreement between Eritrea and Ethiopia and the situation of human rights for people from Eritrea – in the country, on migration routes and in the diaspora. The conference coincided with the EU Summit which discussed a multi-annual financial package for migration.

Adoption of Declaration: Call to stop Human Trafficking in Eritrea, Sudan and Libya and ensure that the migrants in Europe and Israel are properly welcomed

One of the main outcomes of the conference was adoption of the conference Declaration and its submission to the European Union. The Declaration strongly condemned the continued lack of improvements in Eritrea, the involvement of officials in trafficking networks, the torture involved in human trafficking and the policies with which the EU is trying to tackle the problem under the Khartoum Process. The statement urgently called upon the European Union and African Union, as well as the international community, to, among other things, seek reforms in Eritrea – that includes ending the indefinite national service, unconditionally freeing all political prisoners and implementing the Constitution – so that Eritrean refugees can safely return to their homeland. The statement was delivered to the External Action Service of the EU for delivery to the High Representative of the European Union, Federica Mogherini.

Demonstration in Brussels, 14 December 2018

Following the conference, a demonstration was held in front of the European Commission building, where the European Council was rounding up its meeting on the EU budget, during which migration was a topic for discussion. The demonstration asked the EU to stop giving money to governments accused of severe human rights abuses and aiding human trafficking, such as the regimes of Sudan, Eritrea and the Libyan coast guard.

Roundtable: Inhumane treatment and Trafficking of people in Libya: EU and EU Member States' Responsibility

On 1 April 2019, a Roundtable was held in the European Parliament. The event was hosted by Members of the European Parliament (MEPs) Marie-Christine Vergiat (GUE/NGL Group) and Ana Gomes (S&D Group) together with EEPA. Speakers in this event were, among others, representatives of Médecins Sans Frontières, Amnesty International, Human Rights Watch, experts on human trafficking, legal experts, a journalist and human rights activists. All panellists mentioned and attested to the horrific living and detention conditions of refugees in Libya. Human rights activist Abraham Tesfai listed known deaths of Eritrean refugees in Libya in a shocking testimony. It showed how many migrants and refugees are dying in the official and unofficial detention centres because of untreated infection, malnutrition, mistreatment (such as beatings, electrical shocks and rape), machine guns, or even because they commit suicide.

Finally, human rights activists and defenders based in Italy and Germany have recently sorganied a cycling event and demonstration on 6 May 2019 in Brussels in order to follow up on an advocacy campaign which aims to stop EU financing of the Libyan coast guards, and demands the release and evacuation to Europe of refugees from the detention centres immediately, and the overall increased protection of human rights of refugees and migrants in the country.

These initiatives show that the people are hungry for peace, they are keen to push for justice, democracy and increased protection of Eritreans in Eritrea, on route, as well as in diaspora.

Habte Hagos
Engaging with international democracies

Introduction

The failure by the Eritrean regime to provide basic rule of law under which Eritreans can live in their homeland and prosper, rather than flee en masse, is the major disaster the country currently faces, and is likely to face for the foreseeable future. The question for those of us in the diaspora is: what can we do to shape Eritrea to become a free and a democratic country, at peace with itself and its neighbours? Eritreans living in Western democracies have a range of options at their disposal.

The priority is to engage with host country democracies. Western parliaments and assemblies are designed to be receptive to influence: the key question is how best to assemble our arguments and target them most effectively. What can we do to ensure an effective advocacy and lobbying?

About Eritrea Focus

Before Eritrea Focus was established, a group of Eritreans and their friends, concerned about the worsening human rights situation in Eritrea, decided to carry out a 'gap analysis' of the diaspora's human rights activities in the UK to identify how their input could be best utilised to maximise impact. It was immediately apparent that there were a large number of groups doing excellent tasks, but they were, in our view, less focused on engagement with decision-makers, such as government ministers and departments, industry leaders (e.g. mining companies) and investment houses or banks. We decided to fill this gap and took engagement with decision-makers as our mission, with a clear objective to be inclusive and transparent in all that we did. We are a non-party organisation, ethnically and religiously inclusive.

Thus, Eritrea Focus was born in September 2014 as a company limited by guarantee, registered with Companies House in England and Wales, to run a professional human rights campaign. The composition of the Eritrea Focus Board of Governors includes: veterans of the war of liberation, journalists and experts on Eritrea, not-for-profit (third sector) professionals, as well as experienced business people. Our aim is to run Eritrea Focus professionally and as if it were a profit-making operation, setting clear objectives with pre-defined Key Performance Indicators (KPIs) for our projects and activities. We aim to be responsive in our communication by, for example, responding to emails within 24 hours of receipt.

Eritrea Focus is largely funded by Eritrean members of its Board of Governors, while its day-to-day operations are carried out by volunteers. Since its inception, Eritrea Focus has called for:

- Immediate and full implementation of the Eritrean Constitution.
- The establishment of democracy with freedom of association, speech and representation.
- Freedom of religion and the right to worship freely without fear or intimidation.
- An end to the open-ended national service and forced labour in mining, government departments and construction industries.
- An end to killings, arrests, false imprisonments and torture.
- The demarcation of the disputed border between Eritrea and Ethiopia in line with the 2002 ruling of the Eritrea-Ethiopia Boundary Commission.

To help achieve its objectives and given its limited resources, Eritrea Focus works in partnership with a number of like-minded organisations, including War on Want,[145] Amnesty International, the anti-slavery group Freedom United,[146] the London Mining Network (an alliance of human rights, development, environmental and solidarity groups[147]), Publish What You Pay (a group of civil society organisations that advocate for financial transparency in the extractive industry[148]) and the Assenna Foundation, which operates an independent radio station, TV channel and website.

Engagement in the UK and notable achievements

Having identified a lack of effective engagement with UK parliamentarians and decision-makers, Eritrea Focus began to explore the various possible channels for both reaching and influencing these audiences. Of these channels, the All-Party Parliamentary Group on Eritrea has proven successful both in engaging a broad spectrum of parliamentarians and giving exposure to a wide range of critical issues in Eritrea.

---

145   https://waronwant.org/what-we-do
146   https://www.freedomunited.org/
147   http://londonminingnetwork.org/about/
148   https://en.wikipedia.org/wiki/Publish_What_You_Pay

All-Party Parliamentary Group on Eritrea

All-Party Parliamentary Groups, or APPGs, are cross-party groups formed by MPs and Members of the House of Lords who join together to pursue a particular topic or common interest. Due to their non-partisan approach to issues, and the fact that they comprise members from both Houses of Parliament, they can be influential.

The APPG on Eritrea was established in March 2016. Baroness Kinnock played a major part in the formation of the APPG – it would not have been possible to set up the APPG without her tireless drive and influence. Subsequent to the formation of the APPG, Baroness Kinnock served as a Vice-Chair, steadfastly championing for the cause of the Eritrean people. Baroness Kinnock stepped down from the APPG in 2018 due to ill health, but her enthusiasm and dedication continue to resonate within the group and its members.

The purpose of the APPG on Eritrea is to raise awareness of the human rights abuses that are taking place in Eritrea; to examine and debate how the human rights situation in the country might be improved; and to raise matters of concern with, and make representations to, the UK government and other policy makers.

Eritrea Focus acts as the Secretariat for the APPG on Eritrea. Currently, as of January 2019, the officers are:

- Co-Chair Dr David Drew (Labour);
- Co-Chair Thangam Debbonaire (Labour);
- Patrick Grady (Scottish National Party);
- Ann Clwyd (Labour);
- Jeremy Lefroy (Conservative);
- Sir Henry Bellingham (Conservative);
- Lord Alton of Liverpool (Crossbench).

Since the APPG was first formed, parliamentary business has largely been dominated by the issue of the UK's withdrawal from the EU, consuming a significant portion of MPs' time and capacity. Despite this, engagement with the parliamentarians has been consistent, and solid foundations have been laid for the future growth and activity of the group.

Eritrea Focus has also worked with and contributed to other All-Party Groups, including the APPGs focusing on human rights, religious freedoms and Sudan.

APPG on Eritrea meetings

The APPG has provided a platform for discussions on a wide range of topics relating to Eritrea in a parliamentary setting. It is able to attract the highest-ranking individuals and leading international experts from a wide range of prominent institutions, including but not limited to: the UN and the Economist. The following are examples of some of the meetings held by the APPG:

- **The plight of Eritrean asylum seekers in the UK**: keynote speech from Martin Plaut on plight of asylum seekers; update on G11 prisoners; border dispute with Ethiopia; British mining companies in Eritrea; Dutch defamation case against Mirjam Van Reisen.
- **The Eritrean Exodus:** speakers were: Dr John Campbell (SOAS); Lisa Doyle, Head of Advocacy at the Refugee Council; Selam Kidane, Eritrea Focus, Diaspora Representative and University of Leiden; Karl Pike, Refugees and Asylum Policy Manager at British Red Cross.
- **Effect of Eritrean government policies on the economy:** speakers were: Charlotte King, Senior Africa Analyst at the Economist Intelligence Unit; Professor Gaim Kibreab, Professor and Course Director of Refugee Studies, London South Bank University.
- **Briefing from Sheila B Keetharuth, UN Special Rapporteur on the Situation of Human Rights in Eritrea:** this meeting heard from Ms Keetharuth while she was still in post as the Special Rapporteur. Sheila discussed her work on the Commission of Inquiry on Human Rights in Eritrea, her role in reporting on human rights abuses in Eritrea and her extended mandate to follow-up on the Commission's final recommendations. She outlined her findings, including that it is likely the Eritrean regime has committed crimes against humanity. While in London Ms Keetharuth also had private meetings with the Home Office and Foreign Affairs Select Committee, which at that time was examining the FCO's involvement in Eritrea.
- **Reporting on Eritrea: The role of domestic and international media:** speakers were: Francesca Unsworth, Director of the BBC World Service (now of BBC News); Solomon Mugera, Head of BBC Africa; and Michela Wrong, journalist and author. The meeting was held as the BBC World Service launched its Tigrinya service.
- **EU migration policy in the Horn of Africa: Searching for sustainable solutions to people smuggling and trafficking:** speakers were: Duncan Hill, Deputy Head, East and West Africa Departments, Foreign and

Commonwealth Office; Dr Lucy Hovil, Senior Research Associate, International Refugee Rights Initiative; Caitlin Chandler, Journalist and Writer and Editorial Board Member, Africa is a Country; and 'Experts by Experience', Daniel (from Eritrea) and Yacoub (from Sudan). This meeting was a joint session of the APPGs for Sudan and South Sudan; Refugees; and Eritrea.

- **Religious persecution in Eritrea: A crime against humanity:** speakers were: Lord Alton of Liverpool; Dr Berhane Asmelash on the persecution of Evangelical Protestants; Sheikh Mohamed Juma Aburashed on the persecution of Muslims; Fr Shenouda Haile on the persecution of Orthodox Christians. This meeting was a joint session of the APPGs for Eritrea and for Freedom of Religion and Belief, and organised in partnership with Christian Solidarity Worldwide, OpenDoors and Aid to the Church in Need.

APPG notable successes

Recommendations from APPG sessions include supporting the renewal of the mandate of the UN Special Rapporteur, challenging the normalisation of relations with Eritrea to reduce the refugee flows and encouraging the Ethiopian government to implement the Ethiopia-Eritrea Boundary Commission ruling of April 2002.

APPG members have proactively maintained pressure on the government to take note of the situation in Eritrea. While meetings provide an arena for discussion and analysis, activities via parliamentary instruments such as Early Day Motions and Parliamentary Questions are officially recorded and elicit a government response, which can be useful in revealing the government's position on a certain issue and how this may or may not change over time.

Early Day Motions

Early Day Motions (EDMs) are motions submitted for debate in the House of Commons. They are used to draw the attention of the House to a particular issue, event or campaign, and other MPs can show support for the cause by adding their signature to the EDM. By attracting a significant number of signatures, they can be used to demonstrate the level of parliamentary support for a particular cause.

Since the APPG on Eritrea was launched in 2016, it has tabled two EDMs, both of which were signed by MPs from across the House. The first of these was in June 2016, when then-APPG Chair Patrick Grady tabled a motion calling on the House to acknowledge the findings of that year's UN Commission of Inquiry on Human Rights in Eritrea, and urging the government to 'publicly denounce these gross violations of human rights, do everything in its power to ensure protection for Eritreans fleeing these appalling conditions and support victims of the regime as they seek justice'. The motion was signed by 37 MPs from across all main opposition parties, as well as a Conservative backbencher.

A further EDM tabled that year, again by Patrick Grady, acknowledged Eritrea's brutal system of indefinite national service and expressed MPs' concern for Eritrean asylum seekers deported by the Home Office after it was deemed safe for them to return Eritrea, calling on the government to 'immediately change its Country Information and Guidance on Eritrea so those at risk know that they are welcome to seek refuge in the UK'. Signatories once more included a range of MPs from all main opposition parties, demonstrating the broad interest in the government's policies towards Eritrea and Eritrean refugees in the UK.

The full details of both EDMs can be found in **Appendix 6**.

Parliamentary Questions

In addition to these EDMs, since the launch of the APPG in March 2016 over 140 Parliamentary Questions on Eritrea have been tabled and answered by the government, the vast majority of which – about 100 – were raised by officers of the APPG.

A Parliamentary Question, or PQ, is a question put formally by an MP or Peer to a government minister about a matter for which they are responsible. PQs may be asked orally or in writing. Oral questions are put to ministers in person by an MP or Peer in the Chamber/House.

Written questions are used to obtain detailed information about policies and statistics on the activities of government departments. Typically, MPs can expect a response within seven days and Peers within 14 days of the question being tabled.

Responses to PQs sometimes attract media interest. For example, in October 2018, an answer given in response to a written question from Lord Alton on the UK government's assessment of human rights reforms in Eritrea was reported on Africa News, a pan-African English language news website. The article quoted the government's claim that it had seen 'no evidence of any human rights reforms in Eritrea', and also noted Eritrea's contentious election to the UN Human Rights Council the previous week.

PQs have proved to be an important channel for gauging the government's stance on issues relating to Eritrea, and have also been a useful tool for measuring the impact of awareness-raising activities undertaken by Eritrea Focus – as was the case with our report into corporate complicity in human rights abuses in the Eritrean extractive sector.

Notable examples of other parliamentary questions raised by APPG on Eritrea can be found in **Appendix 7.**

Mining and Repression in Eritrea: Corporate Complicity in Human Rights Abuses

In 2018, Eritrea Focus published *Mining and Repression in Eritrea*, a desk-based research report into the extractive sector in Eritrea, believed to be the first of its kind. The report showed the scale of the mining operations in the country, which involve 17 mining companies from across the globe. Chinese, Canadian, Indian and Australian companies are involved in mining or exploration projects, but key roles are also played by UK mining and financial firms. British companies and the City of London are integral to these operations.

The report noted that: 'mining in Eritrea raises important issues for the UK Parliament, particularly in relation to allegations of the use of National Service conscripts in the mining sector. These enforced labourers are, as a UN Commission of Inquiry found, effectively slave labourers. Slavery is illegal under British law, and new provisions in the Modern Slavery Act 2015 put companies under a clear duty to take responsibility wherever it occurs within their supply chains. They must scrutinise and report on their operations and subsidiaries beyond their second, third and fourth tiers with a view to eradicating slavery from their supply chains'.

Eritrea Focus submitted the report to the APPG on Eritrea in June 2018 and made six specific recommendations. Eritrea Focus specifically requested that the APPG 'ask the appropriate government departments what steps are being taken, in the light of the evidence of gross human rights violations, to ensure that measures in accordance with UK Anti-bribery legislation, the Modern Slavery Act, and the Extractive Industries Transparency Initiative are applied to company activities in Eritrea'.

Following the publication of the report, Lord Alton tabled a Parliamentary Question 'To ask Her Majesty's Government what assessment they have made of the recent report by Eritrea Focus to the All-Party Parliamentary Group on Eritrea, Mining & Repression in Eritrea: corporate complicity in human rights abuses, and its implications for Government policy. (HL8640)'.

The government responded, saying that it had 'received the recent report by Eritrea Focus', and that *'Eritrea remains a human rights priority country under the Foreign and Commonwealth Office (FCO) Annual Human Rights Report. The FCO and the British Embassy in Asmara regularly engages with UK companies, and companies with UK investment, involved in the extractive sector in Eritrea. Discussions include their duty to comply with the legislative and regulatory requirements of operating in Eritrea, and the human rights of Eritrean nationals involved in their operations in Eritrea. The British Government will take appropriate action against companies and/or individuals who fail to comply with the relevant.'*

The extractive sector report received a fairly wide media coverage, and the full report is available on our website www. eritrea-focus.org

Eritrea in the news

In addition to this direct parliamentary engagement, Eritrea Focus has also reached out to wider audiences through public events, including seminars and exhibitions. These events have received media coverage and have provided an opportunity to educate and inform people about issues in Eritrea, in the hope that they will be motivated to raise these issues with local politicians or representatives.

One such event was 'Eritrea in the News', a photography exhibition held at the Resource for London throughout September 2018. The exhibition featured more than 50 images – a mix of archive material and personal collections, many never publicly exhibited before – of the places and people that have shaped Eritrea throughout the years.

The photos documented the defeat of Italian occupation forces by British and allied troops in World War Two, and the years of federation of Eritrea with Ethiopia, during which members of the Eritrean Liberation Front (ELF) and Eritrean People's Liberation Front (EPLF) began an armed struggle against Ethiopian rule.

The exhibition also showed the aftermath of independence in 1993, when disputes over border areas led Eritrea and Ethiopia into a devastating new armed conflict in 1998–2000 that killed 100,000 people, and the indefinite conscription that has led many Eritrean refugees to flee their homeland.

Eritrea in the News was inaugurated by Lord Alton of Liverpool, Vice-Chair of the APPG on Eritrea. In his inaugural speech, Lord Alton made reference to the recent session on religious freedoms, telling those present: 'I have heard first-hand testimony from religious leaders of believers being jailed, tortured, and abused in the most heinous ways. While we remain hopeful for the future, it is at such moments that the exposition of Eritrea's past and present become all the more important. The photos you will see here are a reminder of the human stories interwoven in political upheaval and armed conflict. They are a reminder of the desperate conditions that continue to drive many Eritreans to risk their lives fleeing repression, persecution, and enslavement'.

The photos (both digital and in print) are available to individuals and groups who wish to exhibit them. They have already been used in a major conference in Brussels.

Engagement with UK government departments

Eritrea Focus engages with government departments, including the Home Office, the Department for International Development and the Foreign and Commonwealth Office, to discuss prevailing issues in Eritrea and to raise matters of concern such as (a) the illegal 2 per cent levy imposed by the Eritrean government on members of the diaspora, and (b) unprovoked threats and physical attacks on members of the diaspora by PFDJ. These meetings form an integral part of our engagement with UK decision-makers and provide an opportunity to raise important developing issues with those who implement government policies.

International engagement

We have used the international links of our members and supporters to reach out beyond the UK. We now have contacts and friends across Africa, in Europe and the Americas. Bringing you together in this conference is one example of this engagement. We do not intend it to be the last.

Highlight PFDJ violence on members of the diaspora and provide guidance to victims

Eritrea Focus has highlighted attacks by the Eritrean regime in the UK and supported victims of such attacks, including the unprovoked physical attack on the journalist Martin Plaut in November 2018. A guide containing 'A dozen steps on how to peacefully protect human rights activists from PFDJ attacks' was widely circulated and made available on a number of websites.[149]

How can I engage with UK democracy?

A number of channels for engagement with UK parliamentary democracy remain open to members of the Eritrean diaspora, their allies and supporters. These include:

a.   Becoming a member of a progressive political party.

b.   Getting to know your representatives, from your constituency MP to your local councillors, and attending local meetings to network.

c.   Becoming a member of Eritrea Focus to join our activities and receive information about ongoing campaigns and upcoming events, including sessions of the APPG.

d.   Attending sessions of the APPG on Eritrea.

e.   Contacting APPGs such as the APPG on Refugees and APPG on Religious Freedom to be informed of their meetings.

f.   Writing to your MP to encourage them to speak out about the human rights abuses that are taking place in Eritrea.

g.   Identifying peers that are actively interested in human rights, such as religious persecution, and engaging with them.

Conclusion

In Eritrea Focus, we believe there is little to be gained by working in silos, but much to be achieved by working together as a team and in partnership with others. Engagement with international democracies and between members of the diaspora is critically important if we are going to achieve our stated objective to bring rule of law and democracy in Eritrea.

As the old African saying goes: *'If you want to walk fast, walk alone, and if you want to walk far, walk together'.*

Friends, let's walk together for the common good of the Eritrean people. It is through unity that we can remove tyranny from our country. Together we can do it.

149   https://assenna.com/a-dozen-steps-to-peacefully-protect-yourself-from-pfdj-thugs/

12. Next steps, expert groups and concluding remarks

This conference saw a remarkable gathering of people – some Eritreans, others long-term friends of the country. Seldom has so much expertise and goodwill towards Eritrea come together in one place. But no one was left with any doubt about the scale of the challenge that we face. This was clearly laid out at the very start of the conference by Ambassador Haile Menkarios in his written message to the conference.

As he pointed out, Eritrea's history has shaped the task. 'Eritrea's particular history and experience of decolonisation has contributed to the unique nature of governance that has been established there – a one man rather than one party dictatorship.' Ambassador Haile was right. A way must be found that allows the Eritrean people to create the circumstances under which a participatory democracy can replace the current autocracy.

In the two days that we met we heard many important and imaginative contributions. These included calls for women and youth to have their voices heard; for the inclusion of all Eritrea's ethnicities and religions in any transformation and for change to be achieved with the minimum of disruption and the avoidance of violence. All recognised that this will be a hard task. There have been some 52 initiatives for change since 1993: this cannot be allowed to be the 53rd initiative that fails to make a positive contribution to the future of the country.

We were able – through the papers we received, our discussions and debates – to come up with some useful pointers. We recognised that:

1. Change will come from inside Eritrea and be led by Eritreans, who are increasingly desperate for change. In so doing, we need to build on the strength of Eritrean civil society, both inside and outside the country.

2. Religious groups can play a vital role in facilitating the process of change.

3. Ethiopian Prime Minister Abiy Ahmed, while having played a vitally important role in ending the pretext of the disputed border, has no real plan for transforming the region. Ethiopia could disrupt a transformation to democracy, but it cannot lead it.

4. In considering change it might be necessary to opt for a 'soft landing' for members of the regime. This might be difficult for Eritreans to accept, since the suffering has been so intense, but it might be important in healing wounds and moving on.

5. It is vital that we begin to plan and prepare for the transition so that it is as painless as possible.

What can Eritrea Focus do?

Firstly, we accept that we are not a substitute for Eritrean political movements and organisations. Ambassador Haile called for: 'a national conference of representatives of the Eritrean people that would decide on a transitional arrangement to ensure an inclusive process of building participatory democracy in the country'. This is absolutely correct, but it is not a task we can undertake or lead. We can assist, be catalytic and supportive.

Secondly, we must *not* aim for conformity but for collaboration. We accept, encourage and recognise that there are many organisations, including professional groups bringing together Eritrean lawyers and journalists, who have a major role to play. We accept and will work with the existing and emerging civic organisation representing the country's women and its youth. 'Unite, don't harmonise' was a suggested approach and we will continue to reach out to them.

Thirdly, to unite or bring together as many organisations as possible for an inclusive and sustainable change in Eritrea focusing on the big picture of rebuilding a law based functioning democracy post-regime change for the common good of the Eritrean people.

Fourthly, we recognise that there are already a range of resources to facilitate change. These range from the bloggers and social media activists who are now so important in mobilising youth, to the established websites, radio and television stations that are now reaching a growing audience inside the country.

Our ambition

Our plan – working on the issues raised at this conference – is to attempt to undertake two tasks.

The first is to develop a series of working papers which could contribute towards a blueprint for transformation for Eritrea from dictatorship to democracy. These will be written by working groups that reflect the subject areas that were developed at this conference. We will undertake this virtually, but plan to come together in three further, structured conferences, to give them substance.

Secondly, we will attempt to identify and reach out to a diverse group of Eritrean and non-Eritrean experts who could assist in the process of transformation itself. They should be ready to assist in smoothing change, whenever it takes place.

These were the areas we have identified to work in:

	Subject	Lead
1.	Rapprochement between Eritrea and Ethiopia	Martin Plaut
2.	Rule of law and justice	Daniel Mekonnen
3.	Economy and regional integration	Mebratu Ateweberhan
4.	The diaspora, religious groups and youth	Araya Debessay
5.	Engaging international democracies	Mike Slotznick
6.	Lessons from other countries' transitions	Andy Greg
7.	Follow-up conference planning	Habte Hagos

We recognise that this is enormously ambitious, but the need is great and tasks are urgent. They cannot be put aside and wait for more auspicious circumstances. We invite all Eritreans of goodwill to join us in this work.

13. Appendices

Appendix 1: Conference brochure

Building Democracy in Eritrea Conference

Wednesday 24 - Thursday 25 April, 2019

**Senate House
University of London**

Exposing Human Rights Abuses in Eritrea

INSTITUTE OF COMMONWEALTH STUDIES @ 70

SCHOOL OF ADVANCED STUDY UNIVERSITY OF LONDON

Front cover of the conference brochure; available to view here

Appendix 2: Scope of talks

The aim of the conference is to look ahead, rather than dwelling on the past. Whilst it is, of course, important to draw lessons from the past, this should not be the focus of any of the presentations.

1. Winning independence and governing a state

Consider how the birth of Eritrea – so celebrated and so long desired – went so badly wrong. Analyse the factors that led to the current dictatorship, rather than describing the rule of President Isaias. Draw the lessons from this analysis that need to be taken forward to build a country based on law, democracy and constitutional rule.

2. The rapprochement between Ethiopia and Eritrea

The end of the no-war, no-peace confrontation is to be welcomed, but there is a great deal to be done to resolve relationships between the two countries, and across the Horn of Africa. What is the current status of the rapprochement? How should communities along the border be treated? What can Ethiopia legitimately expect in the way of access to the sea, while guaranteeing Eritrean sovereignty? In all this it is important not to allow the Tigrayan people to be targeted as the source of instability, but rather be seen as partners and friends.

3. The rule of law and administration of justice

The failure to live up to the promises made during the liberation struggle to provide a constitutional order under which Eritreans can live and prosper is perhaps the most serious failure of the current regime. But how can the rule of law be brought about once the dictatorship has been removed? Should the Constitution – drawn up and agreed on, but never enacted – be used as the basis for a new order? Or should it be a temporary 'fix' until wider consultations can be held. It will be vitally important to agree on the priority of events. This will have to include the lifting of repression; freedom of expression, assembly and organisation and the holding of free and fair elections. How can this be achieved while maintaining peace and security in a troubled region?

4. The national economy in an integrating region

It was once hoped that Eritrea could be the 'Singapore' of the region, but this has failed to materialise. Instead the nation is trapped in a low growth, peasant-based economy, with few investments beyond the mining sector. Poverty and unemployment have crippled its people, contributing to the exodus abroad.

What measures are required to attract the diaspora to invest and return to the country? How should Eritrea's key geographical position, between a rapidly growing Ethiopia and a wealthy Arab world, be used to the best advantage? Can a free trade regime be established in the region and how would it function? How should laws and regulations be reformed to allow accelerated growth and a drive to prosperity?

5. Eritrean diaspora working together

An assessment of strengths, weaknesses and what can be done to bring the Eritrean diaspora closer together. The mistrust created by the regime in Eritrea has affected opposition groups which has contributed to mistrust between different segments of the opposition, leaving them weak. The lack of trust between civic and political groups has been the biggest challenge. The fact that Eritrean political groups have been ineffectual has been one of the main issues. Despite the weakness created by the mistrust that exists and continues to challenge the opposition there has also been notable work carried out by the opposition.

How can the capacity and robustness of civic organisations be improved to address the needs of Eritrean people? What needs to be done to ensure more effective advocacy and lobbying? How can synergy be created to ensure greater effectiveness? The Eritrean political groups have had very little impact, how can a new political platform be created to ensure that we have vibrant, dynamic, functional political parties who represent all segments of Eritrean society? How to create a more professional opposition? This in itself would improve trust. Have a strategy in place to ensure that all civic groups are going in the right direction and ensure that there is a strong political platform to complement the work of civic organisations.

All the religious groups have suffered under the current regime. Their rights to worship, meet, teach and minister to their people have been restricted. How can all religious groups unite to help reconstruct Eritrean society? What role can they play in healing the terrible wounds inflicted by the conflicts – internal and external – that have plagued the country for so many generations? Can we establish an inter-faith working group to oversee this process?

6. Youth and women's empowerment

Women in Eritrea have become increasingly marginalised, lacking political, social and economic power in the last 27 years due to the repression. Network of Eritrean Women (NEW) is an independent organisation set up by women in the diaspora to fight all forms of discrimination against women and empower them socially, politically, economically and culturally.

The youth in the diaspora have difficulty in setting up viable groups due to the experiences that many have faced. Eritrean Youth Solidarity for Change (EYSC) was one of the groups who fought for change in Eritrea from the diaspora.

What frameworks need to be set to protect the rights of women and youth? What support do these groups need to be viable? What needs to be set up to address trauma and restitution? How can cooperation and networking be improved with women's and youth groups? What role can women and the youth including refugees play in peacebuilding? What policies are needed to ensure that women and young people are an integral part of society and that their issues and needs are addressed?

7. The media, freedom of expression and the right to information

Eritrea has many fine writers, journalists and publishers. The absence of a lively, flourishing culture can be explained entirely by the repression that currently exists. What is required is a framework that guarantees free expression and debate.

Laws and regulations should encourage this, while preventing hate speech and xenophobia. How is this delicate balance to be struck? What role should there be for state-supported media to ensure a diversity of views prevails and that commercial interests do not predominate? What are the rights of minorities and how can their expression be ensured?

8. Engaging with international democracies

Eritreans living in the diaspora frequently experience intense frustration at their inability to influence the direction of their country for the better and the fragmentation of opposition groups. Although some in the diaspora have turned their backs on Eritrea out of despair and wish to build their futures abroad, most are keenly engaged in the affairs of their homeland and care deeply about its future. The question for those who remain engaged is what they can do to shape Eritrea so that it becomes a free, democratic and harmonious nation – far removed from the dictatorship into which it has sunk. For Eritreans living in the 'near abroad' – the Horn of Africa – the options are limited. But Eritreans who have made their homes in Western democracies, from Australia to Canada, Europe to the United States, have a range of options at their disposal.

The first priority must be reconciliation and working together – to find a means of bringing together those who wish to work in this direction in a way that does not run into the problems that have faced political parties down the years. A non-factional way of working needs to be established that is forward-focused, not attempting to reopen old wounds. It is also vital to be aware of the ongoing attempts by the regime to infiltrate, disrupt and intimidate any alternative source of influence – from whichever quarter it comes. Eritreans should naturally lead, but 'friends of Eritrea' may also play a useful role.

The second priority is to engage with host country democracies and the media – recognising that, since we live in democracies, we have a range of tools at our disposal. Our parliaments and assemblies are designed to be receptive to influence: the key question is how best to assemble our arguments and target them most effectively. This requires getting to know and working with our representatives, whether they are Congressmen and Senators, MPs or EU Members. It is a slow, but very useful exercise.

Appendix 3: Eritrean Expert Groups draft remit

The April 2019 'Building Democracy in Eritrea' conference brought together Eritrean and international activists and experts to 'plan for the endgame' (i.e. to formulate a contingency/transitional plan for the country post-regime change). As such, the conference was the start of an ongoing dialogue and engagement rather than an end in itself.

Post-conference, and given the diverse geographical location of the experts, it is expected that such dialogue and engagements could potentially be done and managed along the following lines:

- Subject-based email group of experts or WhatsApp group.
- Country workshops (UK, Germany, Israel, etc.) feeding to a regional group.
- Regional workshops (USA, Europe and Africa) feeding to a global hub.
- Follow-up conference where the output from the various experts groups can be hammered out further and a roadmap blueprint crafted.

The expertise required to pursue the 'endgame plan' and based on the conference output will be:

Ref	Topic	Description	Lead	Members [To be identified by leads]
1	The rapprochement between Ethiopia and Eritrea	Ongoing monitoring and evaluation of developments. What are the plans of the Eritrean government for the open-ended national service now that the 'no-peace' and 'no-war' scenario between the two countries is removed? How should communities along the border be treated? How can Ethiopia legitimately access the Red Sea? Is there a new threat to Eritrean nationhood in a new 'greater Ethiopia'?	Martin Plaut	
2	The rule of law and administration of justice	How can the rule of law be re-established and the necessary institutions put in place? Should the Constitution be enacted as previously agreed by the National Assembly or a fresh Constitution drawn up? How can administration of justice be reinstated and implemented quickly?	Daniel Mekonnen	
3	The national economy in an integrating region	Can a free trade regime be established in the region and how would it function? How best can international aid be galvanised to create a sustainable economy post-regime change? What measures are required to attract the diaspora to invest and return to their country? What international support will be required to create properly functioning banking and financial institutions? The extractive sector now is the predominate source of revenue stream. Should mining contracts be suspended post-regime change to undertake forensic audit of the contracts themselves and to track down past revenue streams? How can a sustainable fishery sector be developed?	Mebrahtu Ateweberhan	
4	Eritrean diaspora working together, including religious groups, youth and women	How to create a more professional opposition that provides synergy and ensures greater effectiveness and cohesion? What frameworks need to be set up to protect the rights of women and youth? How can cooperation and networking be improved with women's and youth groups? What role can women and the youth, including refugees, play in peacebuilding? How can we unite to bring change in our country now and help rebuild Eritrea?	Araya Debessay	
5	Engaging with international democracies	What needs to be done to ensure more effective advocacy and lobbying? How best can opposition groups engage with decision-makers at executive levels in industries and with ministers in government? What lessons can be learnt from the UK All-Party Parliamentary Group (APPG) on Eritrea? How can diaspora members build synergy and exchange ideas to enhance international engagement more effectively and efficiently?	Mike Slotznick	

Ref	Topic	Description	Lead	Members [To be identified by leads]
6	Lessons from other countries' transitions	Case studies and examples of other countries that transitioned from dictatorship to rule of law-based democracy. What are the lessons for Eritrea and how best can they be replicated?	Andy Gregg	
7	Follow-up conference planning	Raise the necessary funds and organise follow-up conference at the end of 2019/early 2020.	Habte Hagos	

Expected output from Eritrean expert groups

Each of the expert groups will research and develop their respective areas of expertise. Their outputs will be consolidated to form a post-regime change draft blueprint. The draft blueprint will be hammered out at a follow-up conference later in 2019 ahead of a consultative process with other experts and the wider Eritrean communities.

Helen Kidane and Habte Hagos will help coordinate the expert groups' work and provide secretarial support as required.

The papers from each of the expert groups will ideally need to be ready by the end of October to be consolidated into a single document ahead of the conference later in 2019.

Appendix 4: Media reports and feedback

Media activity

Media activity around the conference was exclusively post factum, in consideration of sensitivity and security factors. Contact was made with journalists ahead of the conference to extend invitations, issue embargoed press releases and arrange interviews or features, with the expectation that any coverage would be published or broadcast in the days that followed the conference.

With the benefit of having presentations provided in advance, press releases featuring speakers' remarks were drafted ahead of the conference and either issued under strict embargo to previously identified journalists or augmented with any official conference output and issued following the close of the conference on day two (the afternoon of Thursday 25 April).

Key messaging

The core message of the conference, which was used in all media activity, was that this event is not an 'event' but one step in the process towards the establishment of Eritrea as a democratic state. This was achieved by bringing together Eritreans and members of the international community at what is a critical juncture for the country both regionally and globally.

Engagement with the media was therefore focused around one or two key themes of the conference, with the aim of concentrating our efforts and resources on areas likely to be of particular interest re: the future of Eritrea and how the country will look post-Isaias. The following are examples of such areas:

- Winning independence and governing a state: missed opportunities and lessons learned.
- The rule of law and administration of justice.
- Eritreans working together in the country and the diaspora.
- Youth and women's empowerment.

Outcome

We anticipated that our prominent speakers may prove to be a draw for media interest and interviews. Indeed, the involvement of Ambassador Haile Menkerios, and the interest this gathered, demonstrated this. Ambassador Haile's inability to attend ultimately had an undesired impact on our ability to secure as extensive coverage surrounding the conference as we'd hoped. Nonetheless, interviews were successfully carried out with the BBC World Service's Focus on Africa programme, in which journalist Audrey Brown talked about the conference and the current situation in Eritrea with delegates Dr Bereket Habte Selassie and Vanessa Tsehaye. The presence of Assenna TV, together with the extensive coverage it produced in Tigrinya, as well as the interview with Habte Hagos and other delegates, was further advantageous to the conference, and acted as a major catalyst in reaching out to audiences in Eritrea.

Media coverage

Online coverage

Date	Title	Outlet	Link
19/05/2019	The London Building Democracy in Eritrea Conference and the unwarranted criticism it stirred	Assenna	https://assenna.com/the-london-building-democracy-in-eritrea-conference-and-the-unwarranted-criticism-it-stirred/
27/04/2019	The London conference stirs controversy	Awate	http://awate.com/london-conference-stirs-controversy/
10/05/2019	Tigrayans divide Eritrean opposition	African Intelligence	https://www.africaintelligence.com/ion/corridors-of-power/2019/05/10/tigrayans-divide-eritrean-opposition,108356558-bre
28/04/2019	Charting a way forward for Eritrea	Ethiopia Insight	https://www.ethiopia-insight.com/2019/04/28/charting-a-way-forward-for-eritrea/
26/04/2019	Charting a way forward for Eritrea	Eritrea Hub	https://eritreahub.org/charting-a-way-forward-for-eritrea
28/04/2019	The Eritrean government's response to the 'Building Democracy' Conference	Eritrea hub	https://eritreahub.org/the-eritrean-governments-response-to-the-building-democracy-conference
28/04/2019	Charting a way forward for Eritrea	Assena	https://assenna.com/charting-a-way-forward-for-eritrea/
30/04/2019	The Eritrean government's response to the 'Building Democracy in Eritrea' Conference	Eritrea Focus	https://eritrea-focus.org/the-eritrean-governments-response-to-the-building-democracy-in-eritrea-conference/
29/04/2019	A Way Forward for Eritrea	Institute of Commonwealth Studies	https://commonwealth-opinion.blogs.sas.ac.uk/2019/a-way-forward-for-eritrea/
11/05/2019	Building Democracy in Eritrea Conference	Snitna	http://www.snitna.com/articles/Building-Democracy-in-Eritrea-Conference-London-24-to-25-Apr-2019.php
26/04/2019	ምህናጽ ዴሞክራሲ ኣብ ኤርትራ ፡ብዛዕባ ኣብ ለንደን ዝተኻየደ ጉባኤ	Voice of America	https://tigrigna.voanews.com/a/%E1%88%9D%E1%88%85%E1%8A%93%E1%8C%BD-%E1%88%B2%E1%88%9E%E1%8A%AD%E1%88%AB%E1%88%B2-%E1%8A%A3%E1%89%A5-%E1%8A%A4%E1%88%AD%E1%89%B5%E1%88%AB-%E1%89%A5%E1%8B%9D%E1%89%A5%E1%88%8D-%E1%88%A3%E1%89%A5-%E1%88%88%E1%8A%95%E1%8B%B0%E1%8A%95-%E1%8B%9D%E1%89%90%E1%89%93%E1%89%8A%90%E1%8B%90-%E1%8C%89%E1%89%A3%E1%8A%A4/4892698.html

Online coverage

Date	Outlet	Title	Link
27/04/2019	Assenna	ምሁራን ዲሞክራሲ ኣብ ኤርትራ ብከተማ ለንደን ተጋቢኦም፡ ብሞያን-ሕበር ምስ Institute of Commonwealth Studies ካብ 24-25 ማ_ርዝ ኣብ ለንደን ዘካየዱ ኔ_ ከላ_ መ_ላ_ ዋ_ ኣገደስቲ ኣበ_ቃ_ ብ_ኣ_ሳ፡ ጎ_ባ፡ ም_ኖ_ ብ_ው_ ተ_ዘ_ው።	https://assenna.com/%E1%88%9D%E1%88%85%E1%8A%93%E1%8C%BD-%E1%8B%B2%E1%88%9E%E1%8A%AD%E1%88%AB%E1%88%B2-%E1%8A%A3%E1%89%A5-%E1%8A%A4%E1%88%AD%E1%89%B5%E1%88%AB-%E1%89%A5%E1%8B%9D%E1%89%A5%E1%88%8D-%E1%89%B4%E1%88%9B-eritr/

Broadcast

Date	Outlet	Title	Link
26/04/2019	BBC Focus on Africa	Audrey Brown conducts a radio interview with Dr Bereket Habte Selassie and Vanessa Tsehaye	https://www.bbc.co.uk/programmes/w172wn2q7cpb6l6
26/04/2019	ATV Assenna	Interview conducted by Selam Kidane with delegates of the conference	https://www.youtube.com/watch?v=9MomR6hlldA&t=184s
26/04/2019	ATV Assenna	ATV: ሀንጸት ዲሞክራሲ ኣብ ኤርትራ - ዋዕላ ለንደን – ብ Eritrea Focus – 24-25 April, 2019	https://www.youtube.com/watch?v=_2x6dROpe7A
28/04/2019	ATV Assenna	ATV: ሓጺር መብርሂ ኣብ ወ_በር Eritrea Focus ብዛ_ባ ዋ_ ኑ_ ደ_ክራሲ ኣብ ኤርትራ፡ - 24-25 ማ_ርዝ 2019	https://www.youtube.com/watch?v=LVKJ6_ATdvA
26/04/2019	Voice of America Radio Tigrinya	ምሁራን ዲሞክራሲ ኣብ ኤርትራ ብከተማ ኣብ ለንደን ከተቓ_ ገ_	https://tigrigna.voanews.com/a/%E1%88%9D%E1%88%85%E1%8A%93%E1%8C%BD-%E1%8B%B2%E1%8A%AD%E1%88%AB%E1%88%B2-%E1%8A%A3%E1%89%A5-%E1%8A%A4%E1%88%AD%E1%88%AD%E1%89%B5%E1%88%AB-%E1%88%8D-%E1%88%8D-%E1%8A%A3%E1%89%A5-%E1%88%88%E1%8A%95%E1%8B%B0%E1%8A%95-%E1%8B%9D%E1%89%B0%E1%89%93%E1%8A%90%E1%8B%90-%E1%8C%89%E1%89%A3%E1%8A%A4/4892698.html
11/05/2019	Assenna	**ATV: Building Democracy in Eritrea – Opening Remarks: Habte Hagos, Chair of Eritrea Focus**	https://www.youtube.com/watch?v=0NVXVnYoK0Y&t=521s

Appendix 5: Conference feedback

Here is some of the conference feedback received.

Positive feedback

I am humbled and benefited a lot in learning from the resourceful papers presented on the Building Democracy in Eritrea Conference. The conference is timely and a must do. I commend you for organising such a big initiative; I can imagine how much huge burdensome it must have ben to organise.

The conference has triggered uproars by the dictatorial regime and its cronies. This is indicative of the fears the conference has caused to the dictatorial regime in Eritrea. The role of Eritrean Diaspora, as in the past war for liberation years, has a paramount potential and impact in achieving peace and democracy in Eritrea.

As we are all aware, the Eritrean public is desperately looking for the role and guidance of Eritrean intellectuals and those experienced. I therefore, express my appreciation and want to see this initiative continues and flourishes. Linking this initiative to sister initiatives being taken by Eritreans worldwide, would help in bringing a concerted solution to the Eritrean problem. I am sure Eritrea Focus and its partners are aware of this.

YSB/26 May 2019

… hopefully this conference can signal the beginning of the end of dictatorship in our country.

AA/22 May 2019

This was the most professionally organised Eritrean conference I have ever attended.

DS/oral

There has been some 52 previous such conference initiatives over the years, but this was unique in its content and delivery objectives.

CD/Oral

Negative feedback

At the conference a number of delegates expressed concern on diversity, especially pertaining religious groups, women and youth. Following the conference, further concern was expressed by an opposition website that the conference did not fully represent the Eritrean society. Eritrea Focus accepts these constructive criticisms although it was not for lack of trying. Nevertheless, a lesson learned and we will double our efforts to avoid repeat going forward.

AW and others

The breakout sessions were not well organised. This was a point made in the first session and the programme for the rest of the conference was reorganised in the light of the feedback.

Oral

The two-day conference was too short for the depth and breadth coverage of the items set out in the programme and gave very little time for networking. This point is taken and the follow-up conference later this year is expected to be three days rather than two.

Appendix 6: EDMs tabled by members of the APPG

EDM #211, Tabled on 14 June 2016. '2016 Report by UN Commission of Inquiry on Human Rights in Eritrea'. The EDM states:

'That this House notes with concern the findings of the 2016 Report by the UN Commission of Inquiry on Human Rights in Eritrea, published on 8 June 2016; further notes that the Commission describes evidence of crimes against humanity by the Eritrean government, including the use of forced and indefinite military service which the report equates with enslavement; notes that the report details the regime's widespread use of murder, forced disappearance, rape and torture which the regime uses to deter political opposition and instil fear in the population; condemns in the strongest possible terms the systematic human rights violations committed by the Eritrean government as detailed in the report; agrees with the Commission of Inquiry that any and all perpetrators of crimes against humanity should be tried by the International Criminal Court; supports the mandate of the court to investigate any such crimes; and calls on the Government to publicly denounce these gross violations of human rights, do everything in its power to ensure protection for Eritreans fleeing these appalling conditions and support victims of the regime as they seek justice.'

The EDM received 37 signatures. The official Parliament website notes that 'the majority will attract only one or two signatures'. The EDM was sponsored by Patrick Grady (SNP).

EDM #582, tabled on 20 October 2016. 'Upper tribunal (immigration and asylum) decision on asylum seekers from Eritrea'. The EDM states:

'That this House welcomes the decision of the Upper Tribunal (Immigration and Asylum) that Government decisions to return home Eritreans of draft age, who have or might be suspected of having evaded or deserted national service, presents a real risk of persecution or serious harm; notes that Eritrea, sometimes described as Africa's North Korea, is a one-party state accused of appalling human rights abuses against its own citizens, including forced labour, compulsory and indefinite military service and torture; further notes those fleeing that country comprised the largest number of those applying for asylum in the UK in 2015, with 3,695 applicants of which 1,319 applications were granted; is concerned for those already deported by the Home Office which considered it safe for Eritreans to return after leaving the country illegally; agrees with the Home Affairs Committee, which reported in July that the refusal of asylum for such people was unacceptable; and urges the Home Office to immediately change its Country Information and Guidance on Eritrea so those at risk know that they are welcome to seek refuge in the UK.'

The EDM received 31 signatures. It was sponsored by Patrick Grady (SNP).

Appendix 7: Selected PQs raised by members of the APPG

Foreign and Commonwealth Office Written Question
Eritrea: Human Rights
Answered: 23 March 2016

Baroness Kinnock of Holyhead (Labour)

To ask Her Majesty's Government what actions they are taking with regard to claims that Eritreans face human rights violations, in the light of the report by the UN Commission of Enquiry on human rights in Eritrea in June 2015 which concluded that the government of Eritrea engages in abuses that occur in a 'context of a total lack of rule of law' and that it 'is not law that rules Eritreans, but fear'.

Baroness Anelay of St Johns (Minister of State):

The UK recognises the important work of the UN Commission of Inquiry and is concerned by their findings on Eritrea. In particular we are concerned by reports of arbitrary detention, and shortcomings in the rule of law and respect for fundamental freedoms. At the Human Rights Council in July 2015, we supported an extension of the Commission's mandate so that it could continue its work. Bilaterally and through the Human Rights Council we have made clear we want the Government of Eritrea to take concrete action to improve respect for human rights and the rule of law. We have also called on Eritrea to engage fully in Article 8 Dialogue with the EU and cooperate with UN human rights bodies. In May 2015 the Eritrean government announced it would reform the civil, criminal and penal codes. The EU is currently providing funding to help reform local community courts in Eritrea to improve access to justice. The project is working with local community courts to put the reforms of May 2015 into practice.

Foreign and Commonwealth Office Written Question
Eritrea: Mining
Answered: 25 October 2016

Patrick Grady (SNP Chief Whip):

To ask the Secretary of State for Foreign and Commonwealth Affairs, what steps the Government has taken to assist with the implementation of the recommendations put forward to the Human Rights Council by the UN Commission of Inquiry on Human Rights in Eritrea.

Tobias Ellwood (Parliamentary Under-Secretary of State for Foreign and Commonwealth Affairs):

The Government shares the concerns of the UN Commission of Inquiry regarding human rights in Eritrea, in particular shortcomings in the rule of law and indefinite national service.
We have made clear to the Eritrean government the tangible improvements we want to see, including amending its national service system and fully implementing its own Constitution. We are also urging the Government of Eritrea to increase further its engagement with international human rights bodies, such as the UN Office of the High Commissioner for Human Rights, which recently visited Eritrea and was allowed access for the first time to a place of detention. We are supporting UN and EU programmes set up to address recommendations made by the Universal Periodic Review on human rights, and are funding a programme on strengthening the rule of law implemented by the Slynn Foundation.
The mechanism of the Special Rapporteur is an important tool for the international community to strengthen its engagement with Eritrea. The UK Statement to the Human Rights Council on 21 June called on both the Special Rapporteur and the Government of Eritrea to consider ways that they might work together constructively to enhance the progress Eritrea has begun to make in its human rights observance.

Foreign and Commonwealth Office Written Question
Eritrea: Mining
Answered: 25 June 2018

Lord Alton of Liverpool (Crossbench):

To ask Her Majesty's Government what assessment they have made of the recent report by Eritrea Focus to the All-Party Parliamentary Group on Eritrea, Mining & Repression in Eritrea: corporate complicity in human rights abuses, and its implications for Government policy.

Lord Ahmad of Wimbledon (Minister of State):

The Government has received the recent report by Eritrea Focus. Eritrea remains a human rights priority country under the Foreign and Commonwealth Office (FCO) Annual Human Rights Report. The FCO and the British Embassy in Asmara regularly engages with UK companies, and companies with UK investment, involved in the extractive sector in Eritrea. Discussions include their duty to comply with the legislative and regulatory requirements of operating in Eritrea, and the human rights of Eritrean nationals involved in their operations in Eritrea.
The British Government will take appropriate action against companies and/or individuals who fail to comply with the relevant legislation.

Foreign and Commonwealth Office Written Question
Eritrea: Human Rights
Answered: 18 October 2018

Lord Alton of Liverpool (Crossbench):

To ask Her Majesty's Government whether they have seen any evidence of substantive Human Rights reforms in Eritrea since the most recent report of the UN Special Rapporteur on the Situation of Human Rights in Eritrea to the thirty-eighth session of the United Nations Human Rights Council.

Lord Ahmad of Wimbledon (Minister of State):

The UK has seen no evidence of any human rights reforms in Eritrea since the last session of the United Nations Human Rights Council. The Minister for Africa raised our concerns on the human rights situation with the Eritrean Foreign Minister when they met on 25 September, and expressed our hope for an improvement in light of political developments in the region.

Foreign and Commonwealth Office Written Question
Eritrea: Human Rights
Answered: 18 October 2018

Lord Alton of Liverpool (Crossbench):

To ask Her Majesty's Government whether they have seen any evidence of substantive Human Rights reforms in Eritrea since the most recent report of the UN Special Rapporteur on the Situation of Human Rights in Eritrea to the thirty-eighth session of the United Nations Human Rights Council.

Lord Ahmad of Wimbledon (Minister of State):

The UK has seen no evidence of any human rights reforms in Eritrea since the last session of the United Nations Human Rights Council. The Minister for Africa raised our concerns on the human rights situation with the Eritrean Foreign Minister when they met on 25 September, and expressed our hope for an improvement in light of political developments in the region.

Foreign and Commonwealth Office Written Question
Eritrea: Human Rights
Answered: 28 March 2019

Lord Alton of Liverpool (Crossbench):

To ask Her Majesty's Government what assessment they have made of the continuing eligibility of Eritrea for consideration under the United Nations Human Rights Council, Agenda Item 4, Human rights situations that require the Council's attention.

Lord Ahmad of Wimbledon (Minister of State):

It was clear from the Universal Periodic Review on Eritrea, conducted in January 2019, that the human rights situation in Eritrea remains of significant concern to the members of the Human Rights Council. We have encouraged the Government of Eritrea to consider fully all the recommendations made as part of that process, and continue to urge their cooperation with the Special Rapporteur. We look forward to her annual report, which will inform the Council's discussions on Eritrea at its 41st session in June.

Foreign and Commonwealth Office Written Question
Eritrea: Human Rights
Answered: 28 March 2019

Lord Alton of Liverpool (Crossbench):

To ask Her Majesty's Government what assessment they have made of the progress achieved by the government of Eritrea towards (1) releasing political prisoners, (2) ending indefinite conscription, and (3) implementing human rights reforms since the rapprochement between the governments of Eritrea and Ethiopia which began in June 2018.

Lord Ahmad of Wimbledon (Minister of State):

We have seen limited progress on these reforms since June 2018. These issues were raised at the Universal Periodic Review on Eritrea in January and most recently at the Article VIII dialogue discussions between EU Heads of Mission and the Government of Eritrea on 20 March.

Foreign and Commonwealth Office Written Question
Eritrea: Human Rights
Answered: 1 April 2019

Lord Alton of Liverpool (Crossbench):

To ask Her Majesty's Government whether they support the mandate of the United Nations Special Rapporteur on the situation of human rights in Eritrea; and what assessment they have made of the case for continued monitoring and public reporting of human rights abuses in Eritrea.

Lord Ahmad of Wimbledon (Minister of State):

We have consistently supported the mandate of the Special Rapporteur. It was clear from the Universal Periodic Review on Eritrea, conducted in January 2019, that the human rights situation in Eritrea remains of significant concern to the members of the Human Rights Council. We have encouraged the Government of Eritrea to consider fully all the recommendations made as part of that process, and continue to urge their cooperation with the Special Rapporteur. We look forward to her annual report, which will inform the Council's discussions on Eritrea at its 41st session in June.

Lightning Source UK Ltd.
Milton Keynes UK
UKHW051110301019
352533UK00004B/10/P

9 781912 250301